CHARMING SMALL HOTEL GUIDES

Paris
and around

CHARMING SMALL HOTEL GUIDES

Paris
and around

Edited by
Fiona Duncan & Leonie Glass

HUNTER PUBLISHING

DUNCAN PETERSEN

Conceived, designed and produced by
Duncan Petersen Publishing Ltd

Editorial director Andrew Duncan
Production editor Nicola Davies
Art director Mel Petersen
Designers Christopher Foley and Beverley Stewart
Maps Christopher Foley

This edition published 1999 by
Duncan Petersen Publishing Ltd,
31 Ceylon Road, London W14 0PY

Sales representation and distribution in the U.K. and Ireland by
Portfolio Books Limited
Unit 1C, West Ealing Business Centre
Alexandria Road
London W13 0NJ
Tel: 0181 579 7748

ISBN 1 872576 83 4

A CIP catalogue record for this book is available from the British Library

AND

Published in the USA by
Hunter Publishing Inc.,
130 Campus Drive, Edison, N.J. 08818.
Tel (732) 225 1900 Fax (732) 417 0482

ISBN 1-55650-868-9

Printed by G.Z. Printek, S.A.I., Bilbao

Contents

Introduction

Paris was the very first city to have its own guide in the *Charming Small Hotel* series which now covers more than a dozen countries and regions, including the long-established all-France guide, a guide to Southern France, a France Bed-and-Breakfast guide, and the only guide devoted entirely to hotels in Venice.

Paris is romantic, alluring and memorable. Space in this book can't be bought, so it only lists the hotels which, in our inspectors' opinion, best live up to these expectations. And they *are* inspected: each and every one has been visited.

During their 1999 tour of inspection our team not only recorded the hotels' tangible attributes but also looked for the intangible ones. There is no formal way of measuring the warmth of a welcome, for example, but woe betide any hotelier who forgets how important it is to make their guests feel at home.

Having had a lean time in the mid-1990s, Paris hotels are now flourishing. We're pleased to report that prices have changed little in the past two years and, with only a few exceptions, standards of maintenance and housekeeping remain high.

Which part of Paris to stay in?

If you look at the location maps on pages 22-31, you will notice a huge concentration of hotels on the Left Bank, particularly in Saint-Germain-des-Prés and the Latin Quarter, whose quaint streets, ancient buildings and Bohemian and literary associations make a perfect setting for charming small hotels. Another district with a distinctive character and beautiful buildings is the fourth *arrondissement*, including the Marais and Ile Saint-Louis. Nearby, the Pompidou Centre and Les Halles are famous landmarks, but be aware that the surrounding streets are scruffy and down-market. Business people and tourists who are magnetically attracted to the Arc de Triomphe will find accommodation in the (to our mind) far less atmospheric environment of the Champs-Elysées quarter. But no location in the centre of Paris should be entirely discounted. The city has been beautifully preserved, and every district has its own charm. Don't rule out staying further afield – Montmartre or Gobelins – the prices are lower and the public transport is excellent. Some people may prefer to mix a trip to Paris with a stay in the countryside, and our selection of hotels in the Ile-de-France (the province in whose centre Paris lies) offers that oppportunity.

Our criteria

Although this is a guide to city hotels rather than country hotels, the selection criteria remain the same. We aim to include only those places that are in some way captivating, with a distinctive personality, and which offer a truly personal service. Paris presents us with something of a dilemma, since we cannot be as selective as we may when compiling a country or regional guide. We found many hotels which easily attain our very high standards; but there are a significant number which, though basically recommendable, for one reason or another fall short of our ideal. The descriptions of each hotel makes this distinction clear. Be assured that the hotels in this guide are all, one way or another, true to the concept of the charming small hotel, and that they are the pick of the hundreds of small hotels in Paris. If you find any more, please let us know (see page 158).

Our ideal Paris hotel has a calm, attractive setting in an interesting *quartier*, the building itself is either handsome or historic, or at least has a distinct character. The bedrooms are well-proportioned with as much character as the public rooms below. The decorations and furnishings are harmonious, comfortable and impeccably maintained, and include antique pieces that are meant to be used, not revered. The proprietors and staff are dedicated, thoughtful and sensitive in the pursuit of their guests' happiness – friendly and welcoming without being intrusive. The breakfast should be freshly prepared and well presented. Ideally, the hotel will have less than 30 bedrooms; but this is not a rigid requirement – many hotels with more than 30 bedrooms feel much smaller, and you will find such places in this guide.

In making our selection, we have been careful to bear in mind the many different requirements of readers of this guide. Some will be backpackers; others will be millionaires; and the vast majority will fall between the two. They all have in common their preference for a small, intimate hotel rather than a large anonymous one. Whether the hotel be a one-star hostel or a four-star château, it has been included because it fulfils our criteria.

Charming Small Hotel Guides have made their mark not only because of the places they feature, but for the way in which they are edited, designed and produced. Our entries employ, above all, words; they contain not one symbol. They are written by people with something to say, not a bureaucracy which has long since lost the ability to distinguish the praiseworthy from the mediocre.

Every entry aims to give a definite feel of what it is like to stay in that place. The editorial team is small and highly experienced at assessing hotels, and at noticing all-important details. Although we place great emphasis on consistency, we make use in these guides of reports from readers and urge you to tell us what you think of the places you visit (see page 158).

No fear or favour

This is an independent guide. None of the places featured

has paid for their entry. Beware of imitators who accept a 'small fee' for inclusion.

Pet loves

These are some of the things that stand out for us in many of the hotels at which we stayed. Maybe they will strike you too.

Lovely warm and welcoming reception rooms, with beautiful flower arrangements, working fireplaces and original stone floors.

Ancient, charming and architecturally important buildings, with original staircases, masses of beams and stone-vaulted cellars (often serving as the ubiquitous breakfast room).

Original and very pretty wrought-iron lifts, often rib-ticklingly small.

Bedrooms with splendid views, either of a pretty courtyard or street, or across the roof tops to the famous landmarks.

Comfortable beds and excellent linen.

Spotless and sophisticated marble-clad bathrooms.

Pet hates

Moody or downright rude receptionists.

Claustrophobic stone-vaulted breakfast rooms.

Televisions blaring into empty *salons.*

Shoe-box sized bedrooms.

Bedrooms which are banal and which don't live up to the promise of the reception rooms.

Hideous minibars.

Endless white-tiled bathrooms.

Skimpy tea towels masquerading as bath towels.

Noise pollution, caused as much by the lack of sound-proofed windows as by paper-thin walls. Even in the most tranquil back street, beware the 5-am visit by one of the remarkably assiduous fleet of Parisian street-cleaning vehicles.

Mean breakfasts, consisting of one slightly stale croissant, one pat of butter, one mini pot of jam and a jug of luke-warm coffee. Orange juice 20 francs extra.

How to find an entry

In this guide, hotels appear as either full-page, with colour photographs, half-page, or quarter-page entries. Full-page entries are generally the hotels that we judge most attractive. Half- and quarter-page entries are not, in our opinion, as special, but don't disregard them, particularly if your first choice is full, which can often be the case.

Full-page entries appear first, organized by *arrondissement* (the 20 administrative districts arranged by number into which Paris is divided). Within their *arrondissement,* entries are listed alphabetically. The half- and quarter-page entries follow, arranged in the same way. Our small selection of hotels outside Paris are listed at the end of each section.

How to read an entry
At the top of each entry is a coloured bar highlighting the *arrondissement.* Next comes a heading telling you the name of the district in which the hotel is located – Saint-Germain-des-Prés, Marais, Montparnasse etc. Then comes the name of the hotel. By this means, you can find a hotel in a particular area by simply browsing through the headings at the top of the pages, or by using the maps following this introduction to locate the appropriate pages. To locate a specific hotel, use the indexes at the back, which list the entries alphabetically by name, or refer to pages 12-18, where the hotels are divided into districts.

Fact boxes
The fact box given for each hotel follows a standard pattern; the explanation that follows is for full- and half-page entries – quarter-page entries have less detailed fact boxes.

Tel All French telephone numbers now have ten digits. If you are dialling within France, Paris and Ile-de-France numbers must be prefaced with 01; the rest of France is divided into four regional zones (02-05). If you are dialling from abroad, leave off the 0 at the start of the ten-digit number.

Fax The above also applies to fax numbers. The fax has become a standard and trouble-free way of making and comfirming bookings, especially helpful if your French is not up to a telephone call (although the majority of receptionists speak English, and other languages too).

Location Where it is helpful, we have indicated in which part of the street the hotel is located, and given pointers to where the street can be found on a map. **Parking** If your car can be easily parked in the street of the hotel, we have put 'in street'. If the hotel has its own garage (rare), we have put 'free private'. If the nearest parking is in a public car park, we have put the name of the street where you will find the entrance. **Metro** The nearest stations are listed. **RER** (Réseau Express Régional) is the fast suburban service which consists of three lines crossing Paris. The nearest RER station is listed only if it is within reasonable walking distance (with luggage) of the hotel.

Meals It is very rare to find a small hotel in Paris which serves any meals other than breakfast. Where they do, we indicate it, giving a rough idea of the cost of dinner for one without wine, but not for lunch. Room service is more common, and if it is available, we have mentioned it under 'Meals'. It may range from soft drinks, tea and snacks to a full meal service and alcoholic drinks, sometimes provided by outside caterers – for full details, check with the hotel.

Prices In this guide, we have given room and meal prices in francs, rather than using price bands as in many of the other guides in the series. This is because in Paris there is such a large choice of hotels within such a small area that a precise fix on cost is an essential aid to making a choice of hotel.

The basic prices are per room, and first we give the range, from the cheapest single to the most expensive room in the hotel, be it a double, triple or suite. Where hotels have different tariffs for low and high season, our range is from the cheapest room at the low season rate to the most expensive at the high season rate. We have also given the price of a standard double room so that you can see at a glance what you might be expected to pay. If the room price includes breakfast (rare) we say so; otherwise we give the price of breakfast separately. The price quoted is for continental breakfast, which may be just a simple croissant, bread and coffee or a slightly more elaborate affair. Cooked dishes may also be on offer at a higher price – check with the hotel.

In 1994 a *taxe de séjour* (daily fee) was imposed on Paris hotels by the City Council. At the time of writing, this ranges from three to seven francs, depending on the hotel's tourist category (one to four stars). Some hotels include this tax in their quoted prices, others do not – if you would like to know, check when you book. We have tried to give up-to-date prices, but bear in mind that proprietors might have increased them by the time you come to use this book – always check first.

Please note: prices were correct at time of going to press, but hotels may raise their prices at any time. To avoid unpleasant or embarrassing surprises, *check the cost when making a booking.*

Rooms Under this heading we indicate the number and type – single, double, triple, family and suites – and whether the rooms have baths (usually with shower or shower attachment as well) or just showers. Unless stated, you can assume that the bath or shower room will include a WC and washbasin.

If you have a large number of people to accommodate, do ask the hotel if rooms can be arranged to suit you. Although hotels may have one or two suites, rooms are generally not large, but sometimes connecting rooms are available, often with their own separate entrance. Very often the hotel will be able to supply a third bed in a double or twin room for a supplement. The cost varies, but expect to pay around 100F.

Of the facilities we list in the rooms, in most cases the telephones will be direct-dial. In the most recently renovated hotels you will often find a fax/modem point. Most hotels now have cable or satellite TV in addition to the normal terrestrial channels: check with the hotel as to which foreign channels are available. Unlike other guides in the series, we have not listed central heating as a facility, as all the hotels in the book have this; we do, however, indicate when a hotel has air conditioning. More and more hotels are introducing individual air conditioning units in their rooms – much appreciated in summer, especially August.

Facilities Under facilities we list public rooms, and whether the hotel has a courtyard or garden; also if it possesses a lift.

Credit cards We use the following abbreviations:

AE	American Express
DC	Diners Club
MC	MasterCard (Access/Eurocard)
V	Visa (Barclaycard/Bank Americard/Carte Bleu, etc)

Children This heading is almost redundant in Paris because every hotel in this guide is happy to accept children; however, some are more child-friendly than others. Many of the hotels, being small and delicately furnished, are not necessarily suited to young children; the breakfast-rooms in particular, with their small tables and chairs, can present a problem.

Disabled Paris hotels are not the most suitable for those in wheelchairs. There are steps everywhere, very few ramps, and the lifts are often tiny. Newly built or renovated hotels are now required to provide specially adapted rooms. Where facilities exist, they are indicated.

Pets 'Accepted' means that the hotel is happy to accommodate well-behaved small animals. Sometimes they stipulate that animals are not allowed in public rooms. Often a small daily fee will be charged, in the region of 50-100 francs.

Closed Paris hotels rarely close. A handful shut down for a short period in summer or at Christmas.

The final entry in a fact box is normally the name of the **Proprietor**(s). Where a hotel is run by a manager, we give his or her name instead.

Hotels by area and price

In this list hotels are arranged by district, and price bands given.

Price bands		
	F	standard double room less than 600F
	FF	standard double room 600-900F
	FFF	standard double room more than 900F

District	Hotel Name	Pg. no.	Price band
Bastille Quarter	Hôtel le Pavillon Bastille	89	FFF
Beaubourg Quarter	Hôtel Britanique	107	FF
Bois de Vincennes	Hôtel de la Porte Dorée	136	F
Chaillot Quarter	Hôtel du Bois	139	F
	Au Palais de Chaillot Hôtel	94	F
	Hôtel Régence Etoile	142	FF
	Hôtel Majestic	139	FFF
	Saint James Paris	96	FFF
Champs-Elysées	Hôtel Centre Ville Matignon	130	FF
	Hôtel Elysées-Mermoz	82	FF
	Hôtel Etoile-Maillot	92	FF
	Hôtel Etoile Park	142	FF
	Hôtel Franklin Roosevelt	130	FF
	Hôtel Résidence Lord Byron	131	FF
	Hôtel Mayflower	131	FF
	Hôtel Bradford	133	FFF
	Hôtel Claridge-Bellman	133	FFF
	Hôtel de l'Elysée	81	FFF
	Hôtel Galileo	83	FFF
	Lancaster	84	FFF
	Hôtel Libertel Argentine	93	FFF
	Hôtel San Regis	132	FFF

Hotels by area and price

District	Hotel Name	Pg. no.	Price band
Eiffel Tower Quarter	Hôtel Charles Quinze	138	F
	L'Hôtel du Bailli de Suffren	138	FF
Gobelins Quarter	Le Vert Galant	90	F
Gobelins/ Luxembourg Quarter	Port-Royal-Hôtel	115	F
Les Halles	Grand Hôtel de Besançon	109	FF
	Hôtel Saint-Merry	44	FFF
Ile de la Cité	Hospitel	112	F
Ile Saint-Louis	Hôtel des Deux Iles	39	FF
	Hôtel de Lutèce	112	FF
	Hôtel Saint-Louis	42	FF
	Hôtel du Jeu de Paume	40	FFF
Invalides Quarter	Hôtel Latour-Maubourg	73	FF
	Hôtel de Suède	129	FF
	Hôtel de Varenne	129	FF
Invalides/Eiffel Tower Quarte	Hôtel Saint-Dominique	76	F
	Hôtel Relais Bosquet	128	FF
	Hôtel du Cadran	128	FF
	Hôtel Thoumieux	126	FF
	Hôtel Le Tourville	127	FF
	Hôtel de la Tulipe	127	FF
Invalides/Saint-Germain-des-Prés	Hôtel de Nevers	125	F
Jardin des Plantes Quarter	Le Jardin des Plantes	49	F
Latin Quarter	Hôtel Cluny Sorbonne	115	F
	Hôtel and Restaurant Degrés de Notre-Dame	46	F
	Hôtel Esmeralda	113	F

Hotels by area and price

District	Hotel Name	Pg. no.	Price band
Latin Quarter	Hôtel des Grandes Ecoles	47	F
	Hôtel des Trois Collèges	114	F
	Hôtel des Grands Hommes	48	FF
	Hôtel Résidence Henri IV	113	FF
	Hôtel de Notre-Dame	114	FF
	Hôtel du Panthéon	115	FF
	Hôtel Parc Saint-Séverin	50	FF
	Hôtel Le Colbert	45	FFF
	Libertel Quartier Latin	115	FFF
	Hôtel Les Rives de Notre Dame	51	FFF
	La Vie en Rose	52	FFF
Luxembourg Quarter	Hôtel Perreyve	122	F
	Régent's Hôtel	120	F
Marais	Grand Hôtel Jeanne d'Arc	110	F
	Hôtel de Nice	41	F
	Hôtel de la Place des Vosges	111	F
	Hôtel du Septième Art	111	F
	Hôtel de la Bretonnerie	37	FF
	Hôtel Caron de Beaumarchais	38	FF
	Grand Hôtel Malher	112	FF
	Hôtel Saint-Louis Marais	43	FF
	Hôtel Saint-Paul-Le-Marais	112	FF
	Pavillon de la Reine	36	FFF
Marais/Les Halles	Hôtel Beaubourg	110	F
Monceau Quarter	Hôtel Eber	98	FF

Hotels by area and price

District	Hotel Name	Pg. no.	Price band
Montmartre	Hôtel Ermitage	100	F
	Hôtel Prima Lepic	101	F
	Style Hôtel	143	F
Montparnasse	Hôtel de Blois	137	F
	Hôtel Istria	91	F
	L'Atelier Montparnasse Hôtel	116	FF
	Hôtel Danemark	116	FF
	Hôtel Lenox Montparnasse	137	FF
	Hôtel Raspail Montparnasse	137	FF
	Hôtel Le Sainte-Beuve	67	FFF
Nation	Nouvel Hôtel	136	F
North of Etoile	Hôtel Champerret-Héliopolis	141	F
	Hôtel Flaubert	142	F
	Hôtel de Banville	97	FF
	Hôtel Etoile Péreire	142	FF
	Hôtel de Neuville	99	FF
	Hôtel Regent's Garden	141	FF
Opéra Quarter	Hôtel de Beauharnais	134	F
	Hôtel Chopin	87	F
	Hôtel des Croisés	88	F
	Hôtel du Léman	134	F
	Hôtel Gaillon Opéra	109	FF
	Hôtel Queen Mary	132	FF
	Hôtel de l'Arcade	79	FFF
	Hôtel Beau Manoir	80	FFF

Hotels by area and price

District	Hotel Name	Pg. no.	Price band
Opéra Quarter	Hôtel Lido	85	FFF
	Le Stendhal	109	FFF
Opéra/Montmartre	Hôtel Riboutté-Lafayette	135	F
	Hôtel de La Tour d'Auvergne	135	F
Passy	Le Hameau de Passy	132	FF
	Hôtel Massenet	140	FF
Porte Maillot	L'Hôtel Pergolèse	95	FFF
Saint-Germain-des-Prés	Grand Hôtel des Balcons	56	F
	Hôtel de Beaune	124	F
	Hôtel du Globe	62	F
	Hôtel Louis II	117	F
	Hôtel de Nesle	66	F
	Hôtel du Quai Voltaire	126	F
	Hôtel Saint-André-des-Arts	123	F
	Hôtel de l'Académie	128	FF
	Hôtel Bersoly's Saint-Germain	124	FF
	Crystal Hôtel	122	FF
	Hôtel du Danube	122	FF
	Hôtel de Fleurie	61	FF
	Hôtel Lenox Saint-Germain	74	FF
	Hôtel de Lille	128	FF
	Hôtel des Marronniers	118	FF
	Hôtel d'Orsay	75	FF
	Hôtel Le Régent	120	FF
	Hôtel Saint-Paul	70	FF

Hotels by area and price

District	Hotel Name	Pg. no.	Price band
Saint-Germain-des-Prés	Hôtel de l'Université	77	FF
	Hôtel Verneuil	78	FF
	Hôtel d'Angleterre	54	FFF
	Hôtel d'Aubusson	55	FFF
	Hôtel Buci Latin	57	FFF
	Hôtel Relais Christine	58	FFF
	Hôtel Duc de Saint-Simon	72	FFF
	L'Hôtel	117	FFF
	Hôtel Jardin de l'Odéon	122	FFF
	Hôtel Left Bank	63	FFF
	Le Relais Médicis	118	FFF
	Au Manoir Saint-Germain-des-Prés	65	FFF
	Hôtel Montalembert	125	FFF
	Hôtel de l'Odéon	119	FFF
	Hôtel Prince de Conti	119	FFF
	Le Relais Saint-Germain	68	FFF
	Hôtel Saint-Germain-des-Prés	121	FFF
	Hôtel des Saints-Pères	71	FFF
	La Villa	121	FFF
Saint-Germain-des-Prés/ Latin Quarter	Hôtel du Lys	64	F
	Hôtel Le Clos Médicis	59	FF
	Relais-Hôtel du Vieux Paris	123	FFF
Saint-Germain-des-Prés/ Luxembourg Quarter	Hôtel de l'Abbaye	53	FFF
Saint-Germain-des-Prés/ Montparnasse	Hôtel Ferrandi	60	F
	Hôtel Le Saint-Grégoire	69	FFF

District	Hotel Name	Pg. no.	Price band
Tuileries Quarter	Louvre Montana (Comfort Hôtel)	108	FF
	Hôtel Mansart	34	FF
	Hôtel Prince Albert	108	FF
	Hôtel de la Tamise	108	FF
	Hôtel des Tuileries	35	FF
Tuileries/Beaubourg Quarter	Le Relais du Louvre	33	FF
	Hôtel de la Place du Louvre	107	FF
OUTSIDE PARIS			
Barbizon	Hostellerie Les Pléiades	102	F
	Hôtellerie du Bas-Bréau	144	FFF
Dampierre	Auberge du Château	103	F
Ermenonville	Hôtel Le Prieuré	105	F
Flagy	Hostellerie du Moulin	104	F
Fontaine Chaalis	Auberge de Fontaine	146	F
Fontenay-Trésigny	Le Manoir	145	FFF
Germigny L'Evêque	Hostellerie Le Gonfalon	144	F
Provins	Hostellerie Aux Vieux Remparts	106	F
Saint-Germain-en-Laye	La Forestière	145	FFF
	Le Pavillon Henri IV	146	FFF
Senlis	Hostellerie de la Porte Bellon	146	F

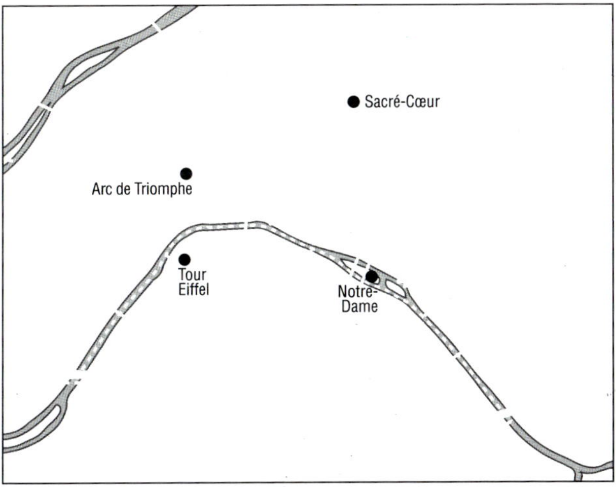

Using the location maps

On pages 22-32 you will find hotel location maps: they show the whereabouts of every hotel in the guide. Both the name of each hotel, and its page number, are shown on the maps.

The scale of the maps is large enough to show every street in which hotels are situated; however it has not been possible to show their precise locations within the streets.

You can use the location maps either to identify a hotel in the particular area or street in which you want to stay, and then turn to its entry; or you can read about a hotel first, then look for its name on the map to learn its whereabouts.

Geography

As we explain in our introduction, page 6, Paris is divided into 20 districts, known as *arrondissements.* They are called *le premier* (written 1er), le deuxième (written 2e) and so on. The hotels in this guide are arranged by *arrondissement,* and the map on this page shows how these lie.

Of course, the different neighbourhoods of Paris are also known by their more familiar names – Latin Quarter, Saint-Germain, Montmartre and so on – and in the hotel entries a sub-heading identifies these areas.

Outside Paris

The map on page 32 shows Ile-de-France, the province in which the city lies, and the locations of our hotel selections surrounding the city. Don't overlook them: many are within easy commuting distance of the city and provide some interesting, often leafy alternatives to staying within the city itself.

Metro map
On page 156-157 you will find a map of the Metro and the RER system.

Useful information
Tourist offices Paris Convention and Visitors Bureau (Office du Tourisme), 127, ave des Champs-Elysées, Paris 75008; tel. (01) 49 52 53 54; open daily 9 am - 8 pm.

Espace de Tourisme Ile-de-France au Carrousel du Louvre, Carrousel du Louvre, 99 rue de Rivoli, Paris 75001; tel. (01) 42 44 10 59; open daily 10 am - 7 pm except Tuesday.

Bureaux de change You will find late-opening *bureaux de change* at the following addresses:

5, rue Ancienne-Comédie, Paris 75006; tel. (01) 43 26 33 30; open daily 9 am - 9 pm.

117, ave Champs-Elysées, Paris 75008; tel (01) 40 70 27 22; open daily 10 am - 10 pm.

Public transport
The RAPT (Paris Transport Authority) operates an efficient and fully integrated network of underground/subway trains, buses and express trains running out into the suburbs. Look out for the route-finder machines providing information on the quickest way to reach your destination by whatever combination of transport suits you. Punch in the relevant data and out will come details of how to proceed.

The Metro
Paris's underground or subway system, officially the Métropolitain, but universally referred to as the Metro, is rightly admired. Service is fast and frequent (trains run at 90-second intervals for much of the day); carriages are generally clean and comfortable; and security, once a problem, is now much improved, with police patrols common at major interchanges (but beware pick-pockets, especially on crowded trains). Smoking is banned throughout the network.

Services start at 5.15 am (a little later on Sunday) and end at about 1.15 am.

Lines are officially numbered but are commonly

known by the names of the stations at either end of the route. These termini names are also used on the orange signs indicating a connection to another line (*correspondence*). The system is easily mastered and clear maps in various formats are available at all Metro stations and at tourist offices.

As stations are close together and few are far underground, you will find the Metro a convenient way of getting about, even for short hops.

The RER

This is Paris's three-line express system – the Réseau Express Régional (RER). The three lines, called A, B and C, are fully integrated into the Metro network but stretch far out into the suburbs, where they run overground, and sometimes in parallel with the SNCF (ordinary rail) suburban services.

The RER lines provide a fast way of getting across Paris, of getting out to the airports and of reaching interesting towns close to Paris such as Versailles or Saint-Germain-en-Laye. Maps are again available from Metro stations and tourist offices.

Buses

The existence of bus lanes on many streets in central Paris means that buses move reasonably fast, except during the evening rush hour. They offer a useful means of seeing Paris, with some positively attractive routes, such as the 24, which takes in the Madeleine, the place de la Concorde, the Louvre, Pont-Neuf, Nôtre Dame and the Latin Quarter.

All buses operate a day-time service from 7 am to about 8.30 pm Monday to Saturday, but only about 20 lines run on Sundays. Some of these also operate an evening service through to about 12.30 am. And ten Noctambus lines, indicated by an owl sign, radiate out from the place du Châtelet between 1.30 and 5.30 am every night. Clear route plans are posted up at bus stops and full bus maps, with lists of evening and Sunday services, are available from Metro stations and tourist offices.

Tickets

The ticketing system for public transport is straightforward and fares are generally value for money. The same yellow tickets are used for both buses and the Metro. The most economical way to buy them is in blocks of ten, called *carnets*, but single tickets are also available, as are a variety of special tourist tickets and passes. They are available from the ticket window at Metro stations and from cafés sporting the RAPT logo.

Hotel location maps

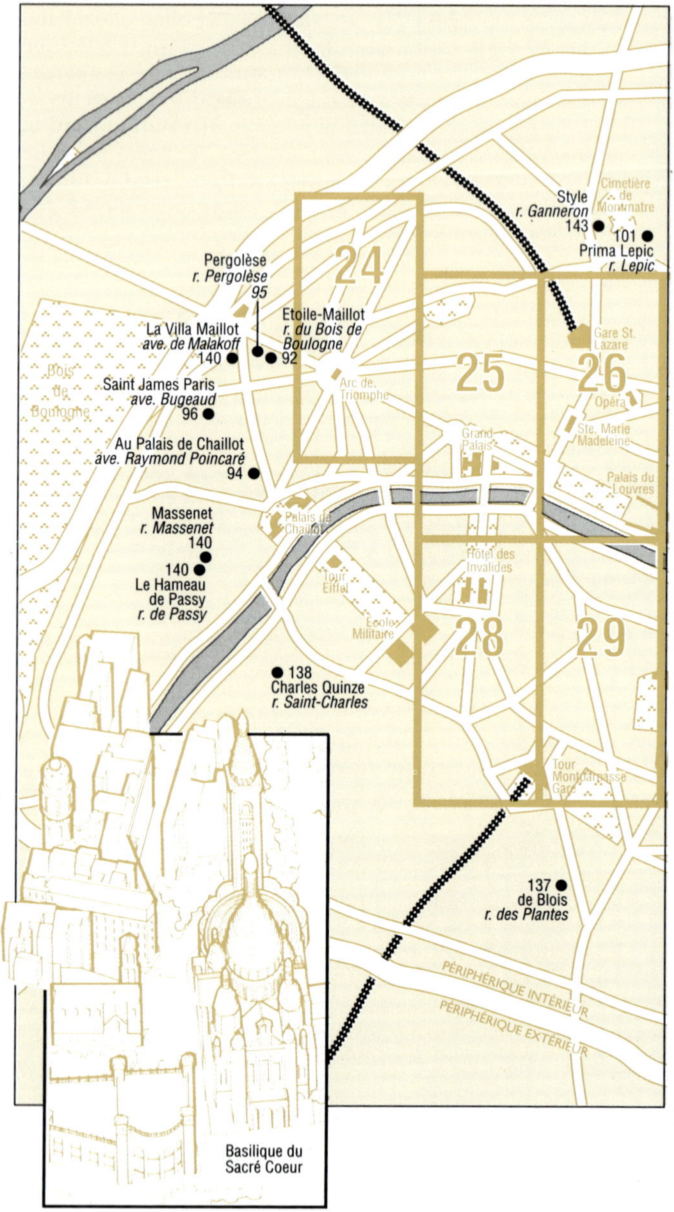

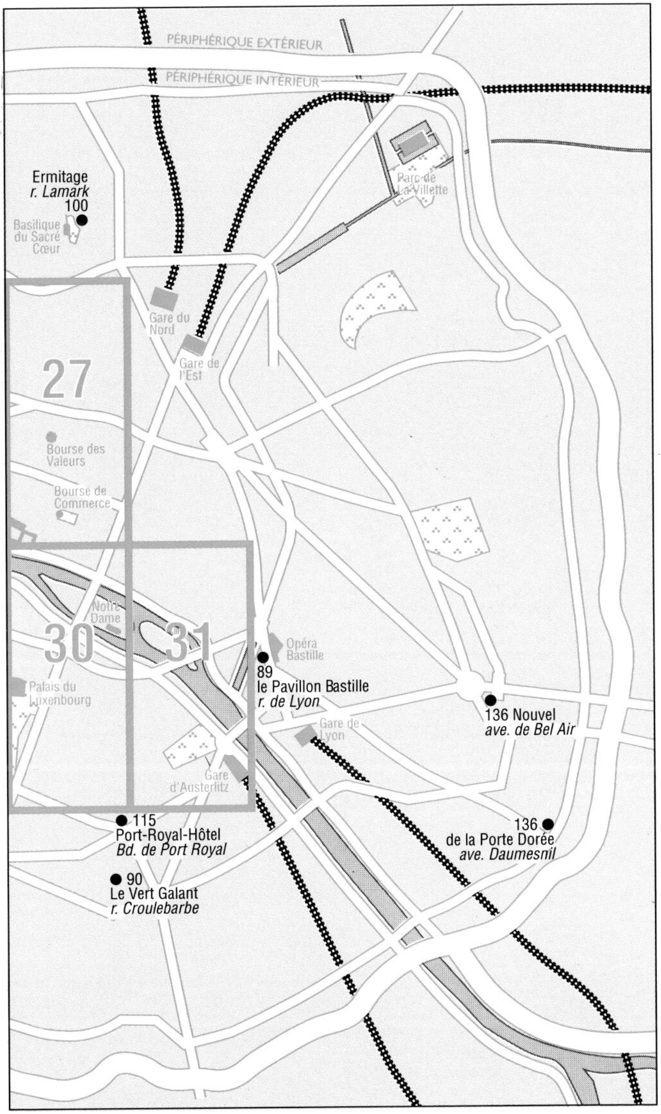
PÉRIPHÉRIQUE EXTÉRIEUR
PÉRIPHÉRIQUE INTÉRIEUR
Ermitage
r. Lamark
100
Basilique du Sacré Cœur
Parc de La Villette
Gare du Nord
Gare de l'Est
27
Bourse des Valeurs
Bourse de Commerce
Notre Dame
30
31
Opéra Bastille
89
le Pavillon Bastille
r. de Lyon
Palais du Luxenbourg
136 Nouvel
ave. de Bel Air
Gare de Lyon
Gare d'Austerlitz
115
Port-Royal-Hôtel
Bd. de Port Royal
136
de la Porte Dorée
ave. Daumesnil
90
Le Vert Galant
r. Croulebarbe

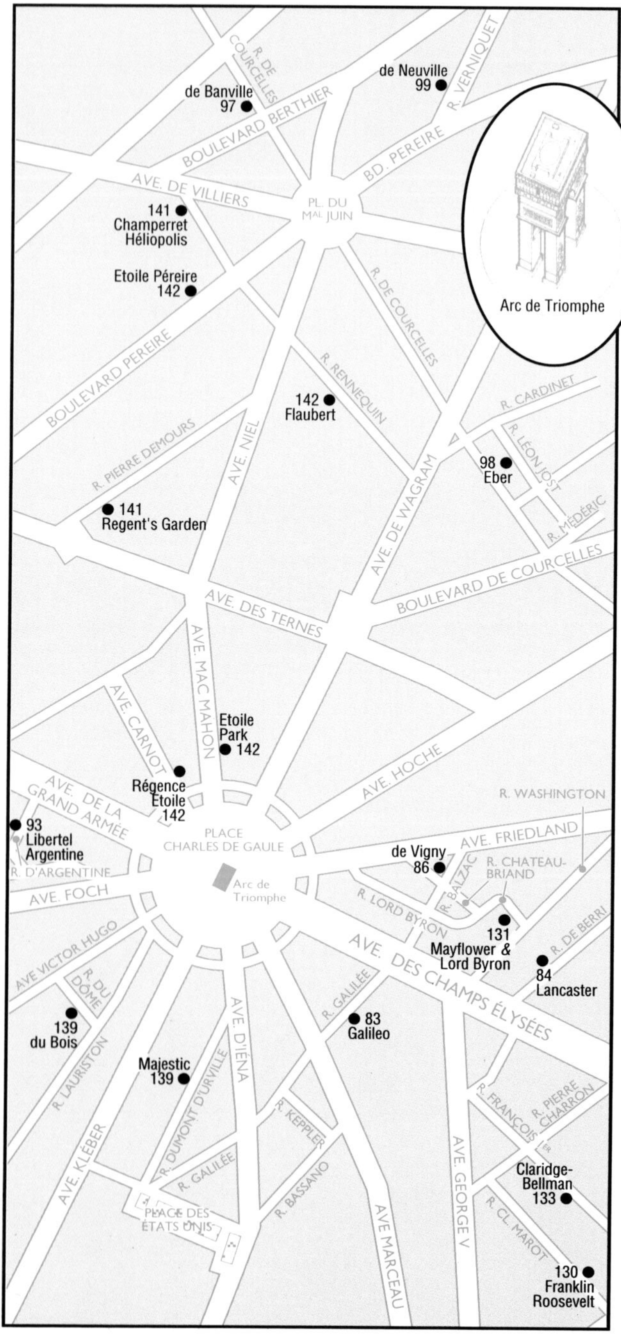

de Neuville
99
de Banville
97
R. DE COURCELLES
BOULEVARD BERTHIER
R. VERNIQUET
BD. PEREIRE
AVE. DE VILLIERS
PL. DU MAL JUIN
141
Champerret Héliopolis
Etoile Péreire
142
Arc de Triomphe
R. DE COURCELLES
BOULEVARD PEREIRE
R. RENNEQUIN
142
Flaubert
R. CARDINET
R. PIERRE DEMOURS
AVE. NIEL
AVE. DE WAGRAM
R. LÉON JOST
98
Eber
141
Regent's Garden
R. MÉDÉRIC
BOULEVARD DE COURCELLES
AVE. DES TERNES
AVE. MAC MAHON
AVE. CARNOT
Etoile Park
142
AVE. HOCHE
Régence Etoile
142
R. WASHINGTON
AVE. DE LA GRAND ARMÉE
93
Libertel Argentine
R. D'ARGENTINE
PLACE CHARLES DE GAULE
AVE. FRIEDLAND
de Vigny
86
R. BALZAC
R. CHATEAU-BRIAND
AVE. FOCH
Arc de Triomphe
R. LORD BYRON
131
Mayflower & Lord Byron
AVE VICTOR HUGO
R. DU DÔME
AVE. DES CHAMPS ÉLYSÉES
R. DE BERRI
84
Lancaster
139
du Bois
R. GALILÉE
83
Galileo
AVE. D'IÉNA
R. LAURISTON
Majestic
139
R. DUMONT D'URVILLE
R. KEPPLER
R. PIERRE CHARRON
R. FRANÇOIS IER
AVE. KLÉBER
R. GALILÉE
R. BASSANO
AVE. GEORGE V
Claridge-Bellman
133
PLACE DES ÉTATS UNIS
AVE MARCEAU
R. CL. MAROT
130
Franklin Roosevelt

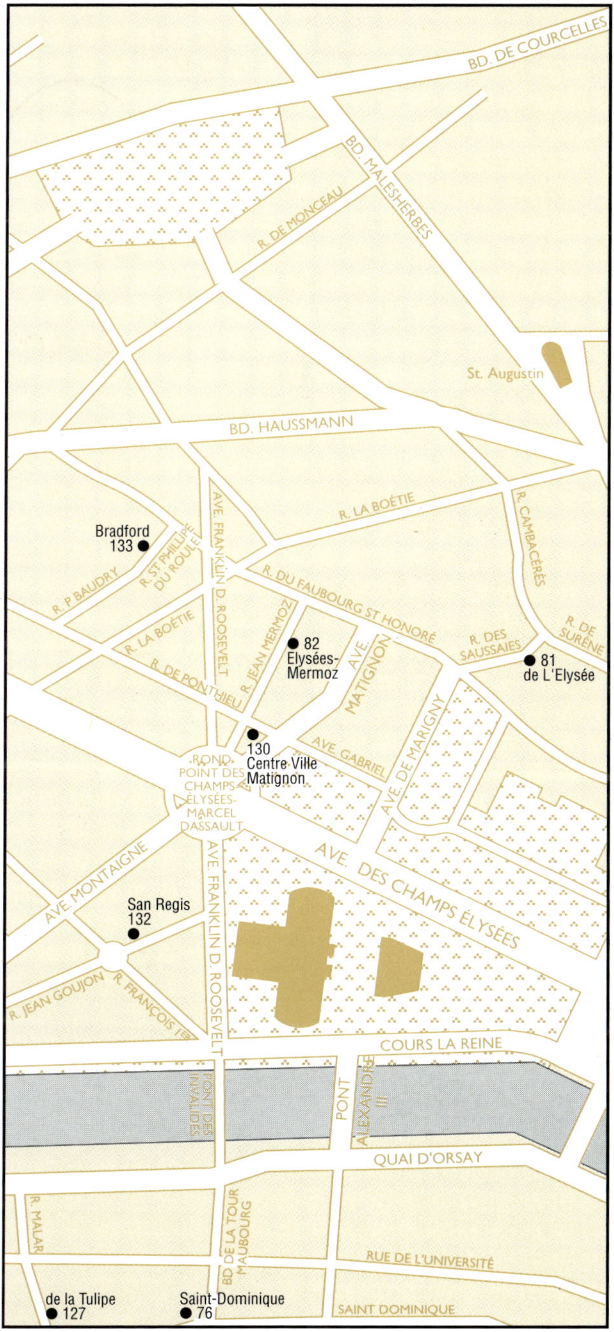
BD. DE COURCELLES
BD. MALESHERBES
R. DE MONCEAU
St. Augustin
BD. HAUSSMANN
R. LA BOÉTIE
R. CAMBACÉRÈS
Bradford
133
R. ST PHILIPPE DU ROULE
AVE. FRANKLIN D. ROOSEVELT
R. P BAUDRY
R. DU FAUBOURG ST HONORÉ
R. DE SURÈNE
R. LA BOÉTIE
R. JEAN MERMOZ
82
Elysées-Mermoz
AVE. MATIGNON
R. DES SAUSSAIES
81
de L'Elysée
R. DE PONTHIEU
AVE. DE MARIGNY
130
Centre Ville
Matignon
AVE. GABRIEL
ROND POINT DES CHAMPS ÉLYSÉES-MARCEL DASSAULT
AVE. MONTAIGNE
AVE. DES CHAMPS ÉLYSÉES
San Regis
132
AVE. FRANKLIN D. ROOSEVELT
R. JEAN GOUJON
R. FRANÇOIS 1ER
COURS LA REINE
PONT DES INVALIDES
PONT ALEXANDRE III
QUAI D'ORSAY
R. MALAR
BD DE LA TOUR MAUBOURG
RUE DE L'UNIVERSITÉ
de la Tulipe
127
Saint-Dominique
76
SAINT DOMINIQUE

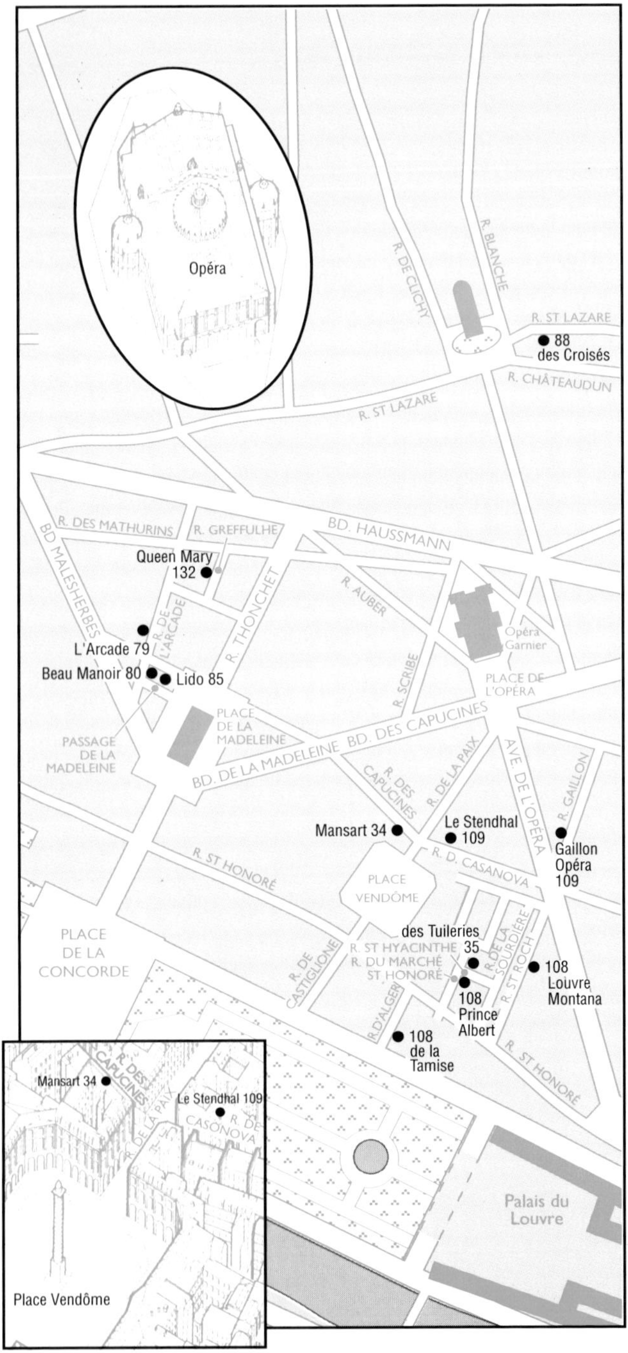
Opéra
R. DE CLICHY
R. BLANCHE
R. ST LAZARE
88
des Croisés
R. CHÂTEAUDUN
R. ST LAZARE
R. DES MATHURINS
R. GREFFULHE
BD. HAUSSMANN
BD. MALESHERBES
Queen Mary
132
R. DE L'ARCADE
R. THONCHET
R. AUBER
Opéra
Garnier
L'Arcade 79
Beau Manoir 80
Lido 85
R. SCRIBE
PLACE DE L'OPÉRA
PLACE DE LA MADELEINE
BD. DES CAPUCINES
PASSAGE DE LA MADELEINE
BD. DE LA MADELEINE
R. DES CAPUCINES
R. DE LA PAIX
AVE. DE L'OPÉRA
R. GAILLON
Mansart 34
Le Stendhal
109
Gaillon
Opéra
109
R. ST HONORÉ
R. D. CASANOVA
PLACE VENDÔME
des Tuileries
35
R. ST HYACINTHE
R. DU MARCHÉ ST HONORÉ
R. DE LA SOURDIÈRE
R. ST ROCH
108
Louvre
Montana
PLACE DE LA CONCORDE
R. DE CASTIGLIONE
R. D'ALGER
108
Prince
Albert
108
de la
Tamise
R. ST HONORÉ
Palais du
Louvre
Mansart 34
R. DES CAPUCINES
R. DE LA PAIX
Le Stendhal 109
R. DE CASONOVA
Place Vendôme

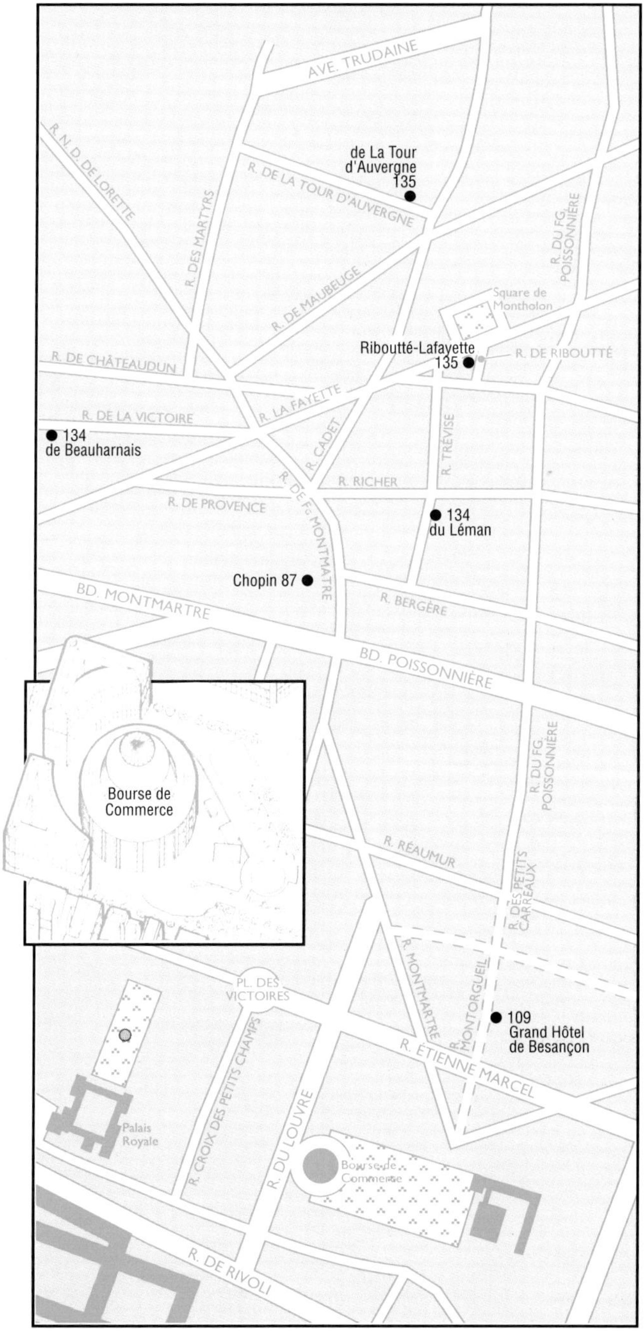
AVE. TRUDAINE
R. N. D. DE LORETTE
R. DE LA TOUR D'AUVERGNE
de La Tour d'Auvergne 135
R. DES MARTYRS
R. DU FG. POISSONNIÈRE
R. DE MAUBEUGE
Square de Montholon
R. DE CHÂTEAUDUN
Ribouttė-Lafayette 135
R. DE RIBOUTTÉ
R. LA FAYETTE
R. DE LA VICTOIRE
134 de Beauharnais
R. CADET
R. TRÉVISE
R. RICHER
R. DE PROVENCE
R. DE Fg MONTMATRE
134 du Léman
Chopin 87
R. BERGÈRE
BD. MONTMARTRE
BD. POISSONNIÈRE
Bourse de Commerce
R. DU FG. POISSONNIÈRE
R. RÉAUMUR
R. DES PETITS CARREAUX
R. MONTMARTRE
R. MONTORGUEIL
PL. DES VICTOIRES
109 Grand Hôtel de Besançon
R. ÉTIENNE MARCEL
R. CROIX DES PETITS CHAMPS
R. DU LOUVRE
Palais Royale
Bourse de Commerce
R. DE RIVOLI

Hotel location maps

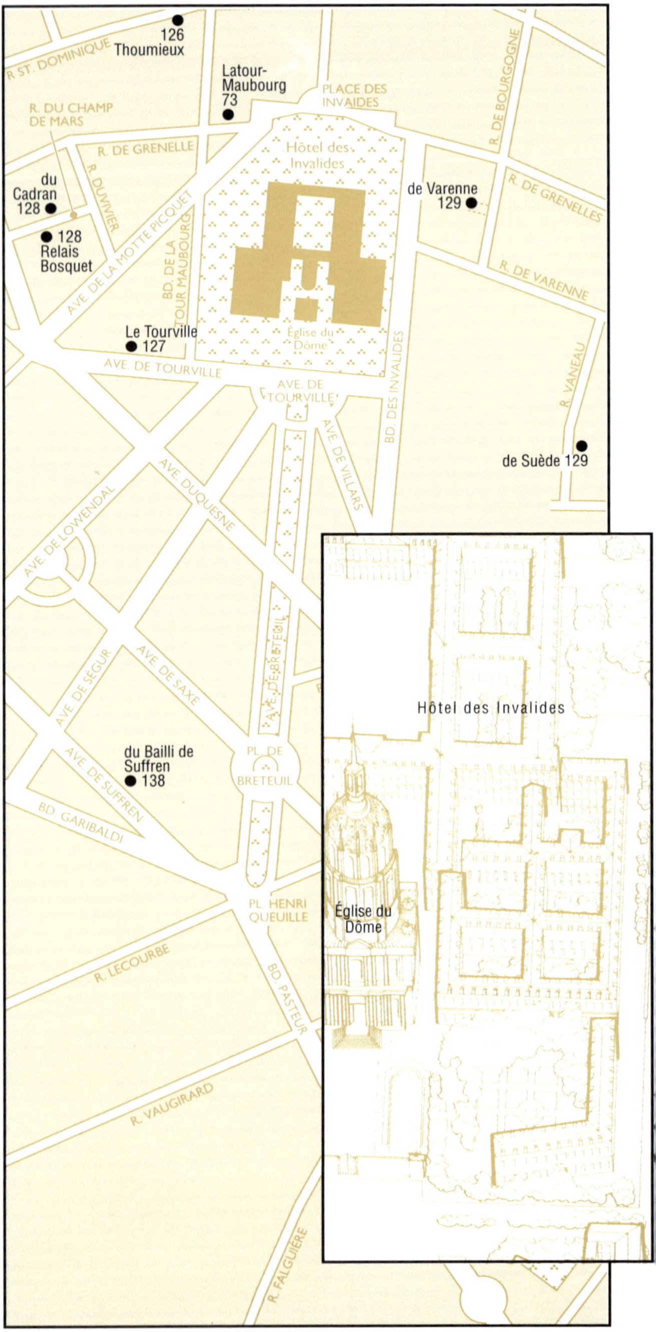

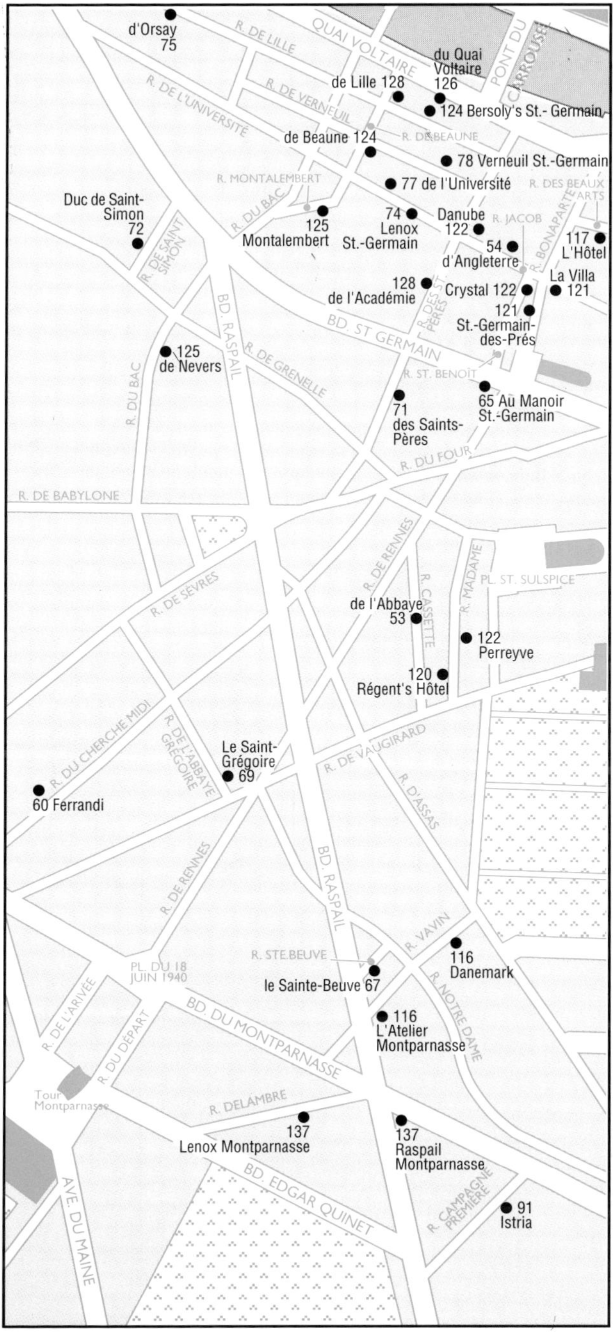
d'Orsay 75
R. DE LILLE
QUAI VOLTAIRE
PONT DU CARROUSEL
du Quai Voltaire 126
de Lille 128
R. DE VERNEUIL
R. DE L'UNIVERSITÉ
124 Bersoly's St.- Germain
de Beaune 124
R. DE BEAUNE
78 Verneuil St.-Germain
R. MONTALEMBERT
77 de l'Université
R. DES BEAUX ARTS
Duc de Saint-Simon 72
R. DU BAC
125 Montalembert
74 Lenox St.-Germain
Danube 122
R. JACOB
117 L'Hôtel
R. BONAPARTE
54 d'Angleterre
R. DE SAINT SIMON
128 de l'Académie
R. DES ST. PÈRES
Crystal 122
La Villa 121
121 St.-Germain-des-Prés
BD. RASPAIL
BD. ST GERMAIN
125 de Nevers
R. DE GRENELLE
R. ST. BENOÎT
R. DU BAC
71 des Saints-Pères
65 Au Manoir St.-Germain
R. DU FOUR
R. DE BABYLONE
R. DE RENNES
R. MADAME
PL. ST. SULSPICE
R. DE SÈVRES
R. CASSETTE
de l'Abbaye 53
122 Perreyve
120 Régent's Hôtel
R. DU CHERCHE MIDI
R. DE L'ABBAYE GRÉGOIRE
Le Saint-Grégoire 69
R. DE VAUGIRARD
R. D'ASSAS
60 Ferrandi
R. DE RENNES
BD. RASPAIL
R. VAVIN
R. STE.BEUVE
116 Danemark
PL. DU 18 JUIN 1940
le Sainte-Beuve 67
R. NOTRE DAME
R. DE L'ARIVÉE
BD. DU MONTPARNASSE
116 L'Atelier Montparnasse
R. DU DÉPART
Tour Montparnasse
R. DELAMBRE
137 Lenox Montparnasse
137 Raspail Montparnasse
BD. EDGAR QUINET
R. CAMPAGNE PREMIÈRE
91 Istria
AVE. DU MAINE

Hotel location maps

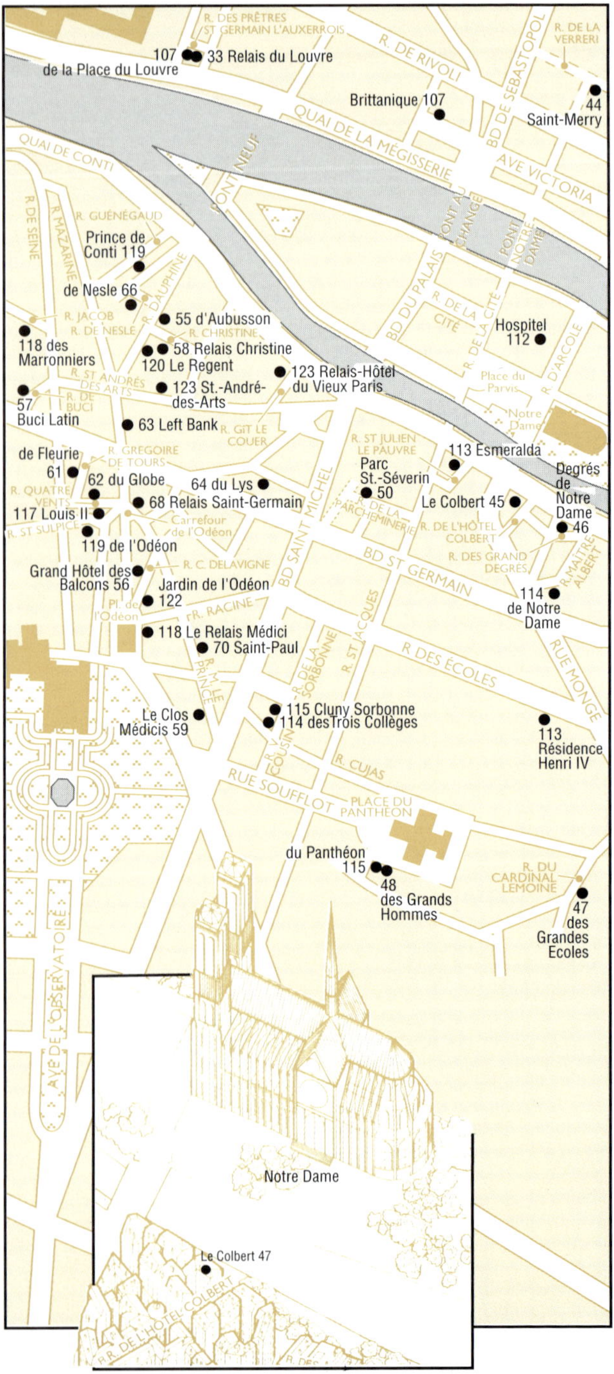

Hotel location maps

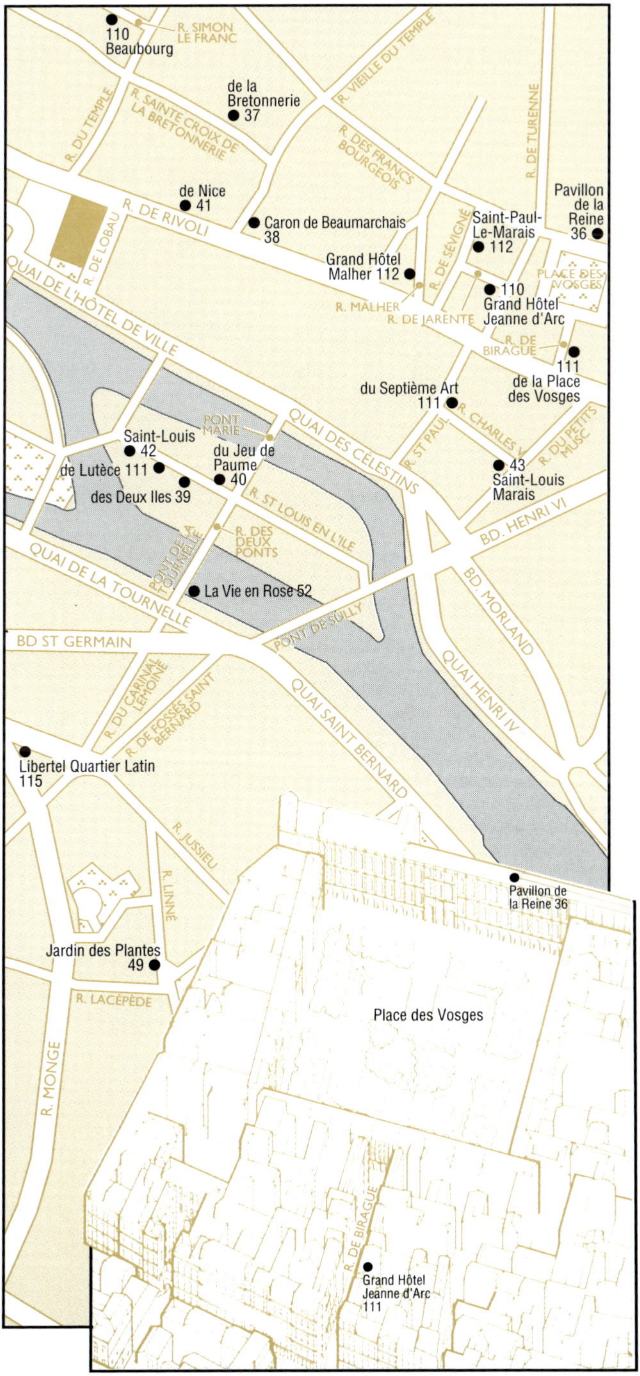

Hotels outside Paris

First Arrondissement

Tuileries/Beaubourg Quarter

Le Relais du Louvre

In a quiet side street hard by the Louvre and the river, this sophisticated little hotel proves that, in the right hands, even the most featureless of bedrooms can be made to feel charming and welcoming. Most are standard box-shape, no more than adequate in size, although some have the benefit of beamed ceilings and floor-length windows. Ours had a terrific view on to the gables and gargoyles of Saint-Germain-l'Auxerrois opposite and, though small, felt extremely welcoming and comforting, with its pink hydrangea curtains and matching bedspread, elegant desk and bedside tables, each with a decent-sized lamp. On the walls were pretty 19thC fashion plates, and the television could be popped away in the upholstered box on which it sat. Breakfast is served in your bedroom.

Rooms are cleverly arranged so that a pair can be taken together, closed off behind a communal front door; two rooms on the ground floor have access on to a little patio. The manageress, Sophie Aulnette, and her close-knit staff pride themselves on trying to accommodate clients in the best way and to help with budgets wherever possible.

Nearby Louvre; Ile de la Cité; Samaritaine store (rooftop view).

19 rue des Prêtres-Saint-Germain-l'Auxerrois, 75001 Paris
Tel (01) 40 41 96 42
Fax (01) 40 41 96 44
Location in quiet side street parallel to Quai du Louvre; **parking** opposite; **metro** Pont-Neuf, Louvre-Rivoli
Meals breakfast
Prices 620-1,500F; standard double 850-980F; apartment 2,200F; breakfast 50F
Rooms 18; 11 double and twin, all with bath; 5 single all with shower; 2 junior suites; all rooms have phone, TV, minibar, hairdrier, safe
Facilities sitting area, lift
Credit cards AE, DC, MC, V
Children accepted
Disabled 2 ground floor bedrooms
Pets accepted
Closed never
Manager Sophie Aulnette

First Arrondissement

Tuileries Quarter

Hôtel Mansart

A stone's throw from the Ritz, spacious bedrooms which recall an earlier, more gracious era, attentive service, fair prices – these are the principal attributes of the excellent Mansart, which was taken over recently by Esprit de France, the group that owns the d'Orsay (page 75) and the Saints-Pères (page 71). When restored, the aged hotel's proportions were left mercifully intact. The large modern lobby, with its expanse of marble floor and walls boldly painted in geometric patterns based on Mansart's drawings for the gardens of Versailles (he was also architect of place Vendôme) is impressive, but it doesn't prepare you for the bedrooms, which you might expect to be similarly contemporary. In fact, though newly decorated, they have a dignified, old-fashioned flavour. We loved No. 205, which feels like a private flat with its own entrance hall opening on to a large room with antique mirrors and regal prints on the white walls, the panelling picked out in gold. The new Italian-tiled bathrooms look the same as those in the group's other hotels. A cheaper option, but equally stately, is No. 212, a huge room with large gilt-framed mirrors and panelled walls – at 900F excellent value, we felt.
Nearby place Vendôme; Opéra Garnier; Tuileries.

5 rue des Capucines, 75001 Paris
Tel (01) 42 61 50 28
Fax (01) 49 27 97 44
Location on corner of place Vendôme; **parking** place Vendôme; **metro** Opéra, Madeleine
Meals breakfast
Prices 900-1,600F; standard double 900F; breakfast 60F
Rooms 57; 53 double and twin, 50 with bath, 3 with shower; 4 single all with bath; all rooms have phone, minibar, TV, hairdrier, safe
Facilities sitting-room, bar, lift
Credit cards AE, DC, MC, V
Children accepted
Disabled no special facilities
Pets not accepted
Closed never
Manager M. Dupaen

First Arrondissement

Tuileries Quarter

Hôtel des Tuileries

This attractive 18thC mansion with Revolutionary associations offers the pleasant combination of a quiet but convenient setting, comfortable accommodation and – perhaps most important in a town where you can't count on it – a genuinely warm welcome. These privileges come at a price however, and our recent inspectors felt that guests were paying over the odds for rooms.

Having said that, the hotel is very well placed both for sightseeing and shopping – close to beautiful place Vendôme and the exclusive shops of rue du Faubourg Saint-Honoré. It has two small salons with velvet seats, paintings and tapestries on plain walls, and Persian rugs on marble floors. There is a small breakfast-room in the basement, and the cellar has been converted into a meeting room for up to 12 people. Bedrooms are individually decorated, often with a bold mix of styles and colours, which almost always comes off. One has a sky-and-clouds theme, another is in Japanese style, another has a four-poster bed and yellow drapes; antique, reproduction and modern furniture is successfully combined. Front rooms are the most elegant and spacious.

Nearby Tuileries; rue de Rivoli; Louvre; place de la Concorde.

10 rue Saint-Hyacinthe, 75001 Paris
Tel (01) 42 61 04 17
Fax (01) 49 27 91 56
Location between rue du Marché-Saint-Honoré and rue de La Sourdière, just N of rue Saint-Honoré; **parking** place du Marché-Saint-Honoré, place Vendôme; **metro** Tuileries, Pyramides
Meals breakfast
Prices rooms 790-1,400F; standard double 890F; breakfast 60F
Rooms 28; 26 double and twin, 2 triple, all with bath; all rooms have phone, TV, air conditioning, minibar, trouser-press, hairdrier, safe
Facilities sitting-room, breakfast-room, lift
Credit cards AE, DC, MC, V
Children accepted
Disabled no special facilities
Pets accepted
Closed never
Proprietor Poulle-Vidal family

Third Arrondissement

Place des Vosges, in the heart of the Marais

Pavillon de la Reine

Set back from the gloriously harmonious Place des Vosges, approached through a calming courtyard garden, the Pavillon de la Reine has our vote for the most perfect location in Paris. Like its sister hotels, the Relais Christine (see page 58) and Saint James (see page 96), it is run with calm professionalism by a dedicated and friendly team, although, like them, perhaps it lacks the intimacy of a truly charming small hotel.

The fine 17thC mansion was once the residence of Anne of Austria, wife of Louis XIII. Rescued from near ruin, it now feels more like a baronial country house, with an impressive entrance hall, handsome panelled sitting-room with comfy leather sofas and a huge stone fireplace complete with roaring log fire, stone-vaulted breakfast-room and two flowery courtyards. For us, the only jarring note was the use of reproduction old masters in some rooms. We were told about the guest of another hotel who removed an expensive original canvas from its frame, replacing it with a copy, but still, we felt it was a misconceived idea.

Upstairs, via a lift cleverly disguised by *trompe l'oeil*, bedrooms contrive to be both smart and pretty, and suitably luxurious.
Nearby Musée Carnavalet; Musée Picasso; Ile Saint-Louis.

28 place des Vosges, 75003 Paris
Tel (01) 40 29 19 19
Fax (01) 40 29 19 20
Location entrance from N side of place des Vosges; **parking** free private garage; **metro** Saint-Paul
Meals breakfast, room service
Prices 1,650-3,500F; standard double 1,800F; breakfast 110F-135F
Rooms 55, all double and twin, including standard, deluxe and junior suites; all with bath; all rooms have phone, TV, air conditioning, minibar, hairdrier
Facilities sitting-room, breakfast-room, 2 courtyard gardens, lift
Credit cards AE, DC, MC, V
Children accepted
Disabled ground floor bedrooms
Pets accepted
Closed never
Manager M. Sudre

Fourth Arrondissement

Marais

Hôtel de la Bretonnerie

A distinctive 17thC townhouse, converted with sympathy and style, which, though conveniently placed in the middle of the picturesque and (now) fashionable Marais district, is – as a recent inspector points out – 'in a rather scruffy street', a little too close to the rowdy atmosphere of the Pompidou Centre. Fortunately, she continues, 'once in the hotel, all is calm and peaceful'.

The exposed beams in the public areas and the upper bedrooms are echoed throughout the house by the sturdy hardwood furniture. The small basement breakfast and sitting-rooms attempt a Medieval flavour, with stone-vaulted ceilings, iron light fittings, richly coloured fabrics and polished tiled floors. Considering the apparent size of the hotel, the bedrooms are surprisingly roomy, also comfortable and pretty, and every one is different; some are arranged with the beds on a mezzanine gallery with the 'downstairs' used as a small sitting area. All have a glossy modern bathroom and guests will find no lack of comfort. Good-humoured staff extend a warm welcome, and cope admirably with such crises as the sudden arrival of all their guests at the same time.

Nearby Hôtel de Ville; Pompidou Centre; Les Halles.

22 Rue Sainte-Croix-de-la-Bretonnerie,
75004 Paris
Tel (01) 48 87 77 63
Fax (01) 42 77 26 78
Location between rue des Archives and rue Vieille du Temple; **parking** Hôtel de Ville (rue de Lobau); **metro** Saint Paul, Hôtel de Ville, Rambuteau; **RER** Châtelet Les Halles
Meals breakfast
Prices rooms 650-1,230F; standard double 630F; breakfast 55F
Rooms 30; 27 double and twin, 3 suites, all with bath; all rooms have phone, TV, minibar, hairdrier, safe
Facilities sitting area, breakfast-room, lift
Credit cards MC, V
Children accepted
Disabled no special facilities
Pets not accepted
Closed end Jul to end Aug
Proprietor M. Sagot

Fourth Arrondissement

Marais

Hôtel Caron de Beaumarchais

The frontage consists of huge plate glass windows surrounded by electric blue paintwork, with the hotel's name emblazoned across the top. A glance inside reveals a square reception *salon* decorated in pretty pink and blue wallpaper with dainty period-style furniture, soft lighting and a huge flower arrangement. As we walked in, we had the fleeting impression that we were entering an upmarket *parfumerie*. The decoration might be a touch too chi-chi for our taste, but once inside, it is impossible not to be caught up in the warmth of this hotel and the staff who run it. Messieurs Bigeard *père et fils* genuinely want their guests to be contented and go to great lengths to ensure that they are.

The hotel's theme is the 18thC – colour schemes are based on the period and fabrics, taken from original designs – but more particularly Beaumarchais (he lived further down the street); there are framed pages from antique editions of the author's most famous work, *Marriage of Figaro*, in each of the small but pretty bedrooms. These have cupboards fronted in fashionable chickenwire and upholstered chairs; some have walk-out balconies. Hand-painted tiles enliven the neat white bathrooms.

Nearby Les Halles; Hôtel de Ville; Notre-Dame.

12 rue Vieille-du-Temple,
75004 Paris
Tel (01) 42 72 34 12
Fax (01) 42 72 34 63
Location close to the rue de Rivoli; **parking** Hôtel de Ville (rue de Lobau); **metro** Hôtel de Ville, Saint Paul
Meals breakfast, brunch
Prices rooms 620-770F; standard double 690F; continental breakfast 54F; brunch 78F
Rooms 19 double and twin, 17 with bath, 2 with shower; all rooms have phone, fax/modem point, TV, air conditioning, minibar, hairdrier
Facilities sitting area, breakfast-room, lift
Credit cards AE, DC, MC, V
Children accepted
Disabled access difficult
Pets accepted
Closed never
Proprietor Etienne and Alain Bigeard

Fourth Arrondissement

Ile Saint-Louis

Hôtel des Deux Iles

As Roland Buffat's well-known converted townhouse moves into its third decade as an archetypical charming small hotel, a couple of recent guests reported a rather 'uncaring' atmosphere during their stay, and felt that complacency had crept in; another was entirely satisfied. We would welcome more comments.

Certainly first impressions are favourable. The inviting sofa and armchairs in the warm and welcoming sitting area have been attractively recovered, although the acres of hessian which cover the walls remain a somewhat dated reminder of the hotel's '70s origins. The plant-filled, glassed-in courtyard which makes such a feature in the lobby looks stunning. Upstairs, the bedrooms are simple and very small, employing Indian prints in warm colours for curtains and bedcovers and again rather dated bamboo bed-heads. Bathrooms are given lift from boldly patterned ceramic tiles hand-painted in blue. (If you have seen as many Paris hotel bathrooms as we have, you will know that it's a positive thrill to see one that isn't uniformly clad in white.) Overall, the effect of the Deux Iles is one of slightly Bohemian warmth, with particularly comfortable public rooms.

Nearby Marais; Notre-Dame; Sainte-Chapelle; Latin Quarter.

59 rue Saint-Louis-en-l'Ile, 75004 Paris
Tel (01) 43 26 13 35
Fax (01) 43 29 60 25
Location in Ile Saint-Louis' main street, between Pont Saint-Louis and rue des Deux Ponts; **parking** Pont-Marie; **metro** Pont-Marie
Meals breakfast
Prices 740-850F; standard double 830F; breakfast 50F
Rooms 17; 12 double and twin, 8 with bath, 4 with shower; 5 single, all with shower; all rooms have phone, TV, air conditioning, hairdrier
Facilities 2 sitting-rooms, breakfast-room, courtyard, lift
Credit cards AE, V
Children accepted
Disabled access difficult
Pets accepted
Closed never
Proprietor Roland Buffat

Fourth Arrondissement

Ile Saint-Louis

Hôtel du Jeu de Paume

We feature no less than four hotels in the delightful rue Saint-Louis-en-l'Ile; but whereas the others are homely, this one is highly original and packs a stylish punch.

As its name implies, the building was the site of a 17thC *jeu de paume* court, built in the days when the 'palm game', forerunner to tennis, was all the rage; when the proprietors acquired it in the 1980s, however, it was a run-down warehouse. Monsieur Prache is an architect and he wrought something of a miracle on the building, opening out the heart of it right up to the roof, exposing all the old timber construction and slinging mezzanine floors around a central well. The impression of light and transparency is reinforced by a glass-walled lift and glass balustrades around the upper floors. Stone walls and all those beams add a reasurringly rustic feel. The sitting area has the appearance of a sophisticated private apartment, with leather sofas, subtle lighting and handsome stone fireplace. Nearby, at the reception desk, the chic, laid-back staff adjust their designer shawls and coolly deal with the guests while a modish sheepdog pads around. Bedrooms are smallish, perfectly pleasant, but nothing like as exciting as the rest of the hotel.
Nearby Marais; Notre-Dame; Latin Quarter.

54 rue Saint-Louis-en-l'Ile, 75004 Paris
Tel (01) 43 26 14 18
Fax (01) 40 46 02 76
Location halfway along the island's main street, near the junction with rue des Deux Ponts; **parking** Pont-Marie; **metro** Pont Marie, Cité
Meals breakfast
Prices 905-2,400F; standard double 1,525F; breakfast 80F
Rooms 32, including suites and duplexes, all with bath and shower; all rooms have phone, TV, minibar, hairdrier
Facilities breakfast-room, sitting-room, bar, courtyard garden, sauna, 2 conference rooms, lift
Credit cards AE, DC, MC, V
Children accepted
Disabled access difficult
Pets accepted (50F per day)
Closed never
Proprietors M. and Mme Prache

Fourth Arrondissement

Marais

Hôtel de Nice

Here is a wonderfully wacky two star, every bit as comfortable and twice as enjoyable as many a more expensive three star. We thought it a terrific find, intrigued and not disappointed by what lay behind the vivid turquoise door and up the winding stairs.

The Nice is the enchanting creation of a previously high-flying professional couple who love both collecting and entertaining. The fruits of their hobby are everywhere – masses of period engravings and prints – particularly of Paris – mirrors, old doors, postcards, even a splendid portrait of Lady Diana Cooper. The effect is charming and highly individual – the panelled *salon*, for example, is a harmony of unco-ordinated colours, fabrics and furniture: antique, painted, modern, garden. The use of wallpaper copied from French 18thC designs makes the compact bedrooms feel fresh and pretty, with the off-beat addition of Indian cotton bedspreads, and doors and skirtings boldly painted in turquoise, orange or pillar-box red. Two attic rooms on the top floor are particularly charming, with their own little balconies. Others look out on to a pretty square. You'll find only basic amenities here, but plenty of character and youthful appeal.

Nearby Musée Carnavalet; place des Vosges; Notre-Dame.

42 bis rue de Rivoli, 75004 Paris
Tel (01) 42 78 55 29
Fax (01) 42 78 36 07
Location near rue Vieille du Temple, on corner of rue de Rivoli and rue du Bourg Tibourg; **parking** Hôtel de Ville (rue de Lobau); **metro** Hôtel de Ville; **RER** Châtelet/Les Halles
Meals breakfast
Prices 380-600F; standard double 450F; breakfast 35F
Rooms 23; 17 double and twin, one family room, all with bath or shower; all rooms have phone, satellite TV, hairdrier
Facilities sitting-room/breakfast-room, lift
Credit cards MC, V
Children accepted
Disabled no special facilities
Pets accepted **Closed** never
Proprietors M. and Mme Vaudoux

Fourth Arrondissement

Ile Saint-Louis

Hôtel Saint-Louis

Ever since its development in the 17thC, Ile Saint-Louis has been one of the most sought-after residential areas in Paris; today it is both chic and picturesque and makes an ideal base for a stay, a peaceful backwater in the heart of the city. Hotels here naturally reflect the superior location in their prices, so if you can't resist, but need to watch the francs, the Saint-Louis makes the best choice. Peering in from the street, the interior looks welcoming, cosy and dignified, with a small but comfortable sitting area; downstairs there is a more than usually attractive stone-vaulted breakfast-room, complete with carved wall fountain and tables laid with pink tablecloths, flowers and pretty china. Renovation work in 1998 has given the Saint-Louis a fresher look. Bedrooms are still best described as dinky with chintz drapes and cane furniture.

The Saint-Louis has a long list of faithful clients, lured by the great location, unchanging standards and warm simplicity of the place. It is sad to note that the friendly 'hands-on' proprietors have bowed to pressure, and revoked their 'no television' policy which used to reinforces the hotel's old-fashioned charm.

Nearby Marais; Notre-Dame; Latin Quarter.

75 rue Saint-Louis-en-l'Ile, 75004 Paris
Tel (01) 46 34 04 80
Fax (01) 46 34 02 13
Location in Ile Saint-Louis' main street, near the Pont Saint-Louis end; **parking** Pont-Marie; **metro** Pont-Marie, Cité
Meals breakfast
Prices 645-845F; standard double 745F; breakfast 49F
Rooms 21 double and twin, 15 with bath, 6 with shower; all rooms have phone, TV, hairdrier, safe
Facilities sitting area, breakfast-room, lift
Credit cards MC, V
Children accepted
Disabled 2 rooms on ground floor
Pets accepted
Closed never
Proprietors Andrée and Guy Record

Fourth Arrondissement

Marais

Hôtel Saint-Louis Marais

This attractive two-star in the heart of the Marais used to be a simple hotel with basic rooms and facilities and a cosy rustic feel. Over the past few years, the Record family have carried out extensive work to upgrade it and a recent inspection revealed a hotel with a rather different style. We felt it was no coincidence that we were greeted by a thrusting young man, one of the new generation of Records, full of ideas for change, who talked of little but websites. To our mind, not all the changes are for the better, for example the arrival of a hideous drinks dispenser in the reception area, which has otherwise been smartened up with Louis XIII-style furniture. The exposed beams, rough-stone walls and terracotta floor still lend a country flavour, which glimpsed from the street through the glazed front door, looks inviting.

Another addition is the cellar breakfast room, a replica of the one in its sister hotel, the Saint-Louis (see page 42). But the most marked changes are in the bedrooms, redecorated in subtle colours or smart stripes, with antique furniture and muted fabrics; tapestry features strongly in wallhangings and upholstered chairs. Some have new sparkling white bathrooms.

Nearby place des Vosges; Musée Carnavalet; Ile St Louis.

1 rue Charles V, 75004 Paris
Tel (01) 48 87 87 04
Fax (01) 48 87 33 26
Location between rue du Petit Musc and rue Beautreillis, S of rue Saint-Antoine; **parking** rue Saint-Antoine; **metro** Bastille, Sully Morland
Meals breakfast
Prices rooms 450-765F; standard double (with shower only) 650-665F; breakfast 45F
Rooms 16 double and twin, all with bath or shower; all rooms have phone, TV, hairdrier, safe
Facilities reception/sitting-room, breakfast room
Credit cards MC, V
Children accepted
Disabled one room on ground floor
Pets accepted
Closed never
Proprietors André and Guy Record

Fourth Arrondissement

Les Halles

Hôtel Saint-Merry

One of the most distinctive small hotels in Paris, the Saint-Merry has a church-like, medieval atmosphere all its own, with heavily beamed ceilings, pale stone walls, wrought-iron fittings and splendid carved wood neo-Gothic furnishings. Everything is kept simple: bedrooms and bathrooms are spotless though mostly small; there are no public rooms to speak of, and breakfast, which is brought to your room, is prepared in a tiny galley behind the reception; a spiralling staircase is the only means by which you can reach your room.

This former presbytery of the adjacent church of Saint-Merri became a private residence after the 1789 revolution, and served for a time as a brothel before it was rescued from decay by its committed proprietor, Christian Crabbe, in the 1960s. He decided on its memorable – if sombre – style after acquiring some neo-Gothic furnishings which were languishing in the basement of the church. The hotel is famous for No. 9, where flying buttresses form a low canopy over the bed, whilst Nos. 12 and 17 have remarkable bedheads. Recently M. Crabbe created a charming suite under the eves.

Nearby Pompidou Centre; Hôtel de Ville; Marais; Notre-Dame.

78 rue de la Verrerie, 75004 Paris
Tel (01) 42 78 14 15
Fax (01) 40 29 06 82
Location in pedestrianized zone, on the corner of rue de la Verrerie and rue Saint-Martin; **parking** Hôtel de Ville (rue de Lobau); **metro** Hôtel de Ville; St Martin; **RER** Châtelet/Les Halles
Meals breakfast
Prices 400-2,400F; standard double with bath 1,000F; breakfast 50F
Rooms 11 double and twin, 3 with bath, 8 with shower, 2 without WC; 2 family rooms, both with shower only; one suite; all rooms have phone, hairdrier
Facilities small sitting area
Credit cards AE, V
Children accepted
Disabled not suitable (no lift)
Pets accepted
Closed never
Proprietor Christian Crabbe

Fifth Arrondissement

Latin Quarter

Hôtel Le Colbert

Set back from the tiny rue Colbert and approached through a wrought-iron gate and imaginatively planted courtyard, Le Colbert gives the impression of a private house rather than a hotel. A handsome building with its origins in the 17thC, it was converted in 1966 into this elegant, well-run three-star hotel which retains its period atmosphere.

On the ground floor, the sunny *salon*-cum-bar with French windows on to the courtyard, ornate upholstered chairs and a host of small tables, is a perfect spot for tea or a drink. Stairs lead down from here to an unusually spacious cellar breakfast-room. A second cosy sitting-room, tucked up under the eaves, boasts a fine view of Notre-Dame.

Many of the bedrooms have floor-to-ceiling windows, *toile de jouy* wallpaper and traditional French-style furniture – velvet chairs and occasional tables; the north-facing rooms have the best views, and there are two fourth-floor suites with beams and sloping walls.

An excellent example of a charming small hotel: it is quiet, has a genuinely friendly staff and is ideally placed for visiting the Ile de la Cité and Left Bank.

Nearby Ile de la Cité; blvd Saint-Germain; Musée de Cluny.

7 rue de l'Hôtel-Colbert, 75005 Paris
Tel (01) 43 25 85 65
Fax (01) 43 25 80 19
Location between quai de Montebello and rue Lagrange; **parking** rue Lagrange, place du Parvis Notre-Dame; **metro** Maubert-Mutualité; **RER** Saint-Michel
Meals breakfast
Prices rooms 890-2,800F; standard double 1,290-1,490F; breakfast 95F
Rooms 36; 34 double and twin, 2 suites, all with bath; all rooms have phone, TV, air conditioning, minibar, hairdrier, safe
Facilities bar/sitting-room, upstairs sitting-room, breakfast-room, conference room, lift **Credit cards** AE, DC, MC, V **Children** accepted
Disabled no special facilities
Pets not accepted
Closed never
Manager Sylvie Alvarez

Fifth Arrondissement

Latin Quarter

Hôtel Degrés de Notre-Dame

Almost all the small hotels of Paris are without a dining-room. Here, however, is an exception – the kind of family-run establishment well-known in the French countryside, but rarely found in the city: a restaurant with rooms. The building is charmingly sited on a little tree-filled square, and the restaurant has the feel of a simple *auberge,* serving correspondingly rustic food, nothing special, but honest. This is where guests also take breakfast (served at any time) which, assures the *patron* (who does not speak English), features the freshest of bread, orange juice squeezed on the spot, and good coffee. A steep wooden staircase (staff carry your bags), decorated with charming murals, leads to the bedrooms, which are good value: well-equipped, with beamed ceilings and smart wooden furnishings. Some rooms have views over Notre-Dame; some are tiny; the ones at the front are the largest, most with triple windows on to the street; No. 24 is handsome, with an expansive desk in the centre. In contrast is the attic conversion, which swaps Gallic character for modern decoration, a private bar and a huge contoured bath. Recent reports from readers have been good.

Nearby Notre-Dame; Musée de Cluny; Ile Saint-Louis.

10 rue des Grands Degrés, 75005 Paris
Tel (01) 55 42 88 88
Fax (01) 40 46 95 34
Location on tiny square at junction with rue Fréderic-Sauton, close to quai de Montebello; **parking** place Maubert; **metro** Saint-Michel; **RER** Saint-Michel
Meals breakfast, lunch, dinner
Prices 380-560F; standard double 490F; breakfast included; dinner: set menus 87-145F
Rooms 10 double, all with bath; all rooms have phone, fax/modem point, TV, hairdrier; some rooms have minibar, fridge
Facilities restaurant, bar
Credit cards MC, V
Children accepted
Disabled not suitable (no lift)
Pets accepted
Closed never
Proprietor M. Tahir

Fifth Arrondissement

Latin Quarter

Hôtel des Grandes Ecoles

Tucked away in a peaceful corner off rue du Cardinal Lemoine and within spitting distance of the Sorbonne, to which its name refers, this hotel is a real find. Its pale pink, shuttered exterior and setting in a lovely courtyard garden lend it the ambience of a country villa. The homely interior is entirely in keeping: a polished wood floor extends from the reception area through to a large breakfast-room, and there is an abundance of mellow wood furniture, rush-seated chairs and lace-covered tables. There are a couple of drawbacks: it has no sitting-room; and the modestly furnished bedrooms have rather immodestly thin walls. Most are decorated with faded flowery fabrics, lace bedspreads and tablecloths. The place exudes old-fashioned charm.

The recent renovation of a second building has given the hotel a further 15 large, bright bedrooms, done out in attractive *toile de jouy* style with fresh-looking bathrooms.

The owner, Madame Le Foch, also runs the hotel, and though she does not speak English, is cheerful and welcoming. A hotel whose simplicity and prices match its two stars, but which has the quiet good taste that few luxury hotels achieve.

Nearby Panthéon; Sorbonne; Musée de Cluny.

75 rue Cardinal Lemoine, 75005 Paris
Tel (01) 43 26 79 23
Fax (01) 43 25 28 15
Location between rue Monge and rue Rollin, S of rue Clovis; **parking** rue Soufflot; **metro** Cardinal Lemoine, Monge
Meals breakfast
Prices rooms 530-690F; standard double 550-590F; breakfast 40F
Rooms 51; 45 double and twin, 6 family, all with bath or shower; all rooms have phone, hairdrier
Facilities breakfast-room, garden, lift
Credit cards MC, V
Children accepted
Disabled 2 specially equipped rooms
Pets accepted
Closed never
Proprietor Mme Le Foch

Fifth Arrondissement

Latin Quarter

Hôtel des Grands Hommes

It's worth putting up with some street noise to have one of the rooms at the front with a view of the Panthéon opposite. Lit up by night, it looks breathtaking – a sight shared by one of des Grands Hommes' two sister hotels, the aptly named du Panthéon (page 115); the other is the Résidence Henry IV (page 113). The best of the three, des Grands Hommes occupies a handsome 18thC building, which retains some original features. The first impression as you walk in is one of warmth, both from the friendly reception staff and from the almost overwhelming peach-coloured decoration: tones vary from the peach panelled walls to deeper apricot chairs and a yellow-hued marble tiled floor. Lush green plants in the minute glassed-in garden provide a splash of contrasting colour. The little cellar breakfast-room, has a low vaulted ceiling (no good for the seriously claustrophobic).

The clever use of pale fabrics makes even the small bedrooms seem light and airy. Some have beams, and some pretty arched French windows. Beds are four-posters or have slightly too shiny brass bedheads. There is one lovely large suite, which sleeps four.

Nearby Panthéon; Saint-Etienne-du-Mont; Sorbonne; blvd Saint-Michel; Musée de Cluny.

17 place du Panthéon, 75005 Paris
Tel (01) 46 34 19 60
Fax (01) 43 26 67 32
Location on S side, between rue Clotaire and rue d'Ulm; **parking** rue Soufflot; **metro** Luxembourg, Cardinal Lemoine, Place Monge; **RER** Luxembourg
Meals breakfast
Prices rooms 600-1,000F; standard double 800F; breakfast 50F
Rooms 32; 31 double and twin, one single, all with bath; all rooms have phone, TV, air conditioning, minibar, hairdrier
Facilities sitting-room, breakfast-room, conference room, lift
Credit cards AE, DC, MC, V
Children accepted
Disabled no special facilities
Pets not accepted
Closed never
Proprietor Mme Moncelli

Fifth Arrondissement

Jardin des Plantes Quarter

Le Jardin des Plantes

From each floor up, you can see a little further into the lovely green oasis of the Botanical Gardens opposite, until you reach the fifth floor, where the rooms not only have the best view, but lead out on to an attractive roof terrace. A botanical theme is carried throughout, from the flower-painted tiles on the reception desk to the buttercup and strawberry lights that illuminate the stairs. The decoration in each of the decent-sized bedrooms is devoted to a particular bloom; walls are covered with green and white trellis paper, dotted with bright yellow mimosa, deep blue irises or pink geraniums. Fabrics co-ordinate, and the chosen flower is picked out in bathroom tiles. With simple, if dated, white cane furniture, the rooms all have a bright summery feel.

Don't be put off by the even more dated decoration downstairs: the cellar sitting-room – a showcase for up-and-coming artists and a musical venue – is pure 1970s brown and beige. This two-star hotel (part of the Timhotel chain), is friendly and comfortable, and offers terrific value. Welcome extras include an ironing room and a sauna. Breakfast is served in the brasserie next door or on the roof terrace.

Nearby Jardin des Plantes; Musée National d'Histoire Naturelle.

5 rue Linné, 75005 Paris
Tel (01) 47 07 06 20
Fax (01) 47 07 62 74
Location opposite NW corner of Jardin des Plantes, between rue des Arènes and rue Lacépède; **parking** rue Censier; **metro** Jussieu, Monge; **RER** Gare d'Austerlitz
Meals breakfast, lunch
Prices rooms 560-630F; standard double 550F; breakfast 49F
Rooms 33; 32 double and twin, one family, all with bath or shower; all rooms have phone, TV, minibar, hairdrier
Facilities sitting-room, brasserie, ironing-room, sauna, lift
Credit cards AE, DC, MC, V
Children accepted
Disabled no special facilities
Pets accepted
Closed never
Proprietor M. Rousseau

Fifth Arrondissement

Latin Quarter

Hôtel Parc Saint-Séverin

Of the many bedrooms described in this book, No. 70 at the Parc Saint-Séverin remains this writer's favourite. And although it's an expensive choice, its assets are far greater than, say, a standard double room at the Pavillon de la Reine (page 36) or the Relais Christine (page 58) which cost some 200F per night more. Overall, of course, those are far superior hotels, but this room is special: a light, sophisticated and beautifully decorated penthouse suite which is entirely encircled by a broad private terrace affording breathtaking views across the rooftops of all the landmark buildings as far as the Eiffel Tower in one direction, Sacré-Coeur in another. Taking breakfast here on a warm summer morning is sheer bliss. Less expensive, but nonetheless very impressive, are two more rooms, each with a broad terrace on three sides. On lower floors, room Nos 50 and 12 both have style and space. The rest are pleasant, unexceptional, pastel coloured, with predominantly grey modern furniture. The large ground floor lobby breakfast-room is a disappointment, another example of contemporary colours – grey, pink, mauve – abstract paintings and minimalist furniture failing to inspire.

Nearby Notre-Dame; Musée de Cluny; Saint-Séverin.

22 rue de la Parcheminerie, 75005 Paris
Tel (01) 43 54 32 17
Fax (01) 43 54 70 71
Location in pedestrian area close to Saint-Séverin and junction with rue des Prêtres Saint-Séverin; **parking** rue Lagrange; **metro** Saint-Michel; **RER** Saint-Michel
Meals breakfast 50F
Prices 500-1,500F; standard double 700F; suite 1,500F; breakfast 50F
Rooms 22 double and twin, one family room, 4 single, all with bath; all rooms have phone, TV, minibar, hairdrier, safe; half are air conditioned
Facilities breakfast-room, sitting area, lift
Credit cards AE, DC, MC, V
Children accepted
Disabled no special facilities
Pets not accepted
Closed never
Manager M. Lebouc

Fifth Arrondissement

Latin Quarter

Hôtel Les Rives de Notre Dame

The brochure speaks of the bureaucracy which almost prevented the owners of this pricey little hotel from transforming the run-down 16thC building which they had bought. Its outlook is the Ile de la Cité across the traffic-heavy quai Saint-Michel and the Seine, but the owners' hearts are firmly in Provence and Tuscany, and the decoration is designed to transport you to the south. In our case, the ground floor reception and glass-and-beam roofed sitting-room managed to take us no further than a fashionable Paris flower shop, thanks to the banks of plants and dried flowers arranged on the tiled floor, the garden-style furniture and the floral collages on the walls.

By contrast, the well-proportioned bedrooms are stylish but less precious than downstairs and have a genuine feel of the sun, with Provençal fabrics, wood-framed windows shaded by the prettiest of white cotton curtains, and charming fabric bedheads held in a frame of verdigris ironwork flowers. All the rooms have a sofa which converts into an extra bed. The bathrooms are attractive, with terracotta floors and lovely basins. Breakfast in bed, brought by uniformed staff, feels like a treat.

Nearby Notre-Dame; Musée de Cluny; Ile Saint-Louis.

15 quai Saint-Michel, 75005 Paris
Tel (01) 43 54 81 16
Fax (01) 43 26 27 09
Location mid-way along quai; **parking** Notre-Dame; **metro** Saint-Michel; **RER** Saint-Michel
Meals breakfast, room service
Prices 995-2,600F; standard double 1,200F; breakfast 85F
Rooms 10; 6 double, 3 single, one suite, all with bath; all rooms have phone, fax/modem point; TV, air conditioning; minibar, hairdrier, safe
Facilities sitting-room, breakfast-room, lift
Credit cards AE, DC, MC, V
Children accepted
Disabled access difficult
Pets accepted
Closed never
Manager Grace Santos

Fifth Arrondissement

Latin Quarter

La Vie en Rose

We couldn't resist including La Vie en Rose in this edition of the guide. It's a charming small hotel with a difference – a barge for two on the Seine. Moored in a prime spot for exploring the Iles and Latin Quarter, it's run by American couple, David Novick and Laura Ann Kamm. They bought the barge – officially *Bateau Jolia* - in 1997, and made their home in the bows. Their guests have the use of a beautifully designed saloon, a luxurious marble bathroom and – down a steep ladder, so not for the elderly or infirm – the stern cabin, panelled in pale wood and containing, according to our reporter, one of the most comfortable beds in Paris. "I loved being rocked to sleep by the river," she says.

Laura's passion for antiques is evident everywhere in the Art Deco furniture, lights and mirrors. It isn't cheap (10,000F for three days), but drinks, snacks, cooked breakfast, museum passes, metro tickets and even long-distance phone calls are all thrown in. David prides himself on his gourmet breakfasts. He'll cook whatever you fancy – eggs, blinis, Toulouse sausage. David and Laura aim to give their guests "what we'd have liked when we came to Paris for a special weekend". And they deliver.
Nearby Ile Saint-Louis; Ile de la Cité; blvd Saint-Germain.

'Bateau Jolia', face au 11 Quai St Bernard, 75005 Paris
Tel (01) 43 54 03 46
Fax (01) 43 29 79 15
Location moored just to the E of Pont de la Tournelle, below Quai de la Tournelle; **metro** Maubert Mutualité; **parking** free parking on quai
Meals breakfast, meals by arrangement
Prices 10,000F for 3 nights, 3,000F for extra night; breakfast included
Room one double room with bath, phone, TV, video, CD player, fax, minibar, tea/coffee kit, hairdrier, safe. No smoking
Facilities sitting-room, sun deck
Credit cards not accepted
Children not accepted
Disabled not suitable
Pets not accepted
Closed never
Proprietors David Novick and Laura Ann Kamm

Sixth Arrondissement

Saint-Germain-des-Prés/Luxembourg Quarter

Hôtel de l'Abbaye

If we gave awards, this gorgeous hotel would be a very strong contender. Indeed, we find it hard to fault with the caveat that the standard bedrooms are fairly small (and feel even smaller compared to the spaciousness of the public rooms); you would do well to upgrade to a larger room if you can. One on the ground floor has its own terrace, as do the four duplex apartments. You need to book well in advance.

The moment we walked into this skilfully converted former abbey, we felt calmed and cossetted. The hotel has a reputation for attentive yet unobtrusive service which it justly deserves: the courteous staff seem genuinely eager to be of help. The public rooms are inviting yet chic, filled with fresh flowers, with several sitting areas, the sofas and armchairs attractively upholstered in floral or striped fabrics, warmly lit by huge table lamps; in cool weather there's an open fire. The breakfast-room/bar must be one of the most alluring in Paris, conservatory style, with walls covered in trellis and French doors which overlook a large courtyard garden complete with fountain. Here you can take breakfast or a drink in warm weather. Worth every penny.

Nearby Jardin de Luxembourg; Saint-Sulpice.

10 rue Cassette, 75006 Paris
Tel (01) 45 44 38 11
Fax (01) 45 48 07 86
Location close to junction with rue de Meziers; **parking** Saint-Sulpice; **metro** Saint-Sulpice
Meals breakfast
Prices 960-1,950F; standard double 980; breakfast included
Rooms 42 double and twin, all with bath; 4 duplex apartments; all rooms have phone, TV, air conditioning, hairdrier
Facilities 2 sitting rooms, breakfast-room/bar, courtyard garden
Credit cards AE, MC, V
Children accepted
Disabled 2 rooms on ground floor
Pets not accepted
Closed never
Proprietors M. and Mme Lafortune

Sixth Arrondissement

Saint-Germain-des-Prés

Hôtel d'Angleterre

One of the most peaceful, comforting and gracious small hotels in Paris, the Angleterre has a faintly English air, befitting a building which was once the British Embassy. In 1783, Benjamin Franklin refused to enter it to sign the Treaty of Paris because he considered it to be British soil. Had he done so, he would have found well-proportioned rooms, fine mantlepieces, a beautiful staircase with *trompe l'oeil* murals and a lovely courtyard garden.

The feeling of spacious calm in the public rooms is echoed in the bedrooms, which are all roomy, elegant and comfortable, often with splendid bathrooms. One guest reports a deluxe room with one of the largest hotel bathrooms he had seen, all marbled and mirrored glamour, based on one in the London Ritz. Another bathroom has a charming hand-painted suite, with the basin set into a wood and tiled washstand. Another couple report that they stayed in the hotel's smallest room – normally let out as a single but with a double bed so that two can share if they wish. Their verdict? Despite the size, they were happy to enjoy the hotel's benefits at a modest price. Their only quibble: the nose-in-air attitude of the receptionists. More recent reports claim that it needs a facelift. **Nearby** blvd Saint-Germain; Musée d'Orsay; Louvre.

44 rue Jacob, 75006 Paris
Tel (01) 42 60 34 72
Fax (01) 42 60 16 93
Location in the stretch of rue Jacob between rue Bonaparte and rue des Saints-Pères; **parking** blvd Saint-Germain (rue du Dragon); **metro** Saint-Germain-des-Prés
Meals breakfast
Prices 650-1,600F; standard double 980F; breakfast 55F
Rooms 24 double and twin, either small, standard or deluxe, all with bath; 3 apartments; all rooms have phone, TV, air conditioning, hairdrier, safe
Facilities sitting-room, breakfast-room, bar, courtyard garden, lift to some rooms only
Credit cards AE, DC, MC, V
Children accepted
Disabled no special facilities
Pets not accepted
Manager Mme Michèle Blouin

Sixth Arrondissement

Saint-Germain-des-Prés

Hôtel d'Aubusson

When our inspector arrived here on a chilly January afternoon, she was greeted by a log fire crackling in the huge grate, focal point of the sitting-room, and a warm welcome from the staff. The go-ahead new manager, Pascal Gimel, is committed to offering faultless service while keeping prices at a reasonable level, convincing us that the Aubusson now deserves a long entry in this guide. It occupies a 17thC honey-stone town house, arranged around a large courtyard. A huge pair of double doors, formally a coach entrance, lead from the street into the airy lobby. To the right, Café Laurent – in various incarnations – has attracted the literati and glitterati since 1690 from Voltaire to Brigitte Bardot. Of the sitting-room, our inspector said, '....my favourite in Paris. It manages to be cosy despite its grand proportions'. It has a high beamed ceiling, Versailles parquet floor and pretty furniture, lamps and mirrors. Appropriately, two Aubusson tapestries hang in the breakfast room next door.

The bedrooms cocoon their inhabitants behind heavy doors in silence and restrained luxury. The most expensive are massive and beamed, but even the smallest are large by local standards. **Nearby** blvd Saint-Germain; Ile de la Cité; Latin Quarter.

33 rue Dauphine, 75006 Paris
Tel (01) 43 29 43 43
Fax (01) 43 29 12 62
Location corner of rue Christine; **metro** St-Michel/Odéon; **parking** private garage
Meals breakfast, light meals, 24 hr room service
Prices 1,050F-2,050F; standard double 1,050-1,350F; breakfast 95F
Rooms 49 double and twin, all with bath; all rooms have phone, TV, fax/modem point, air conditioning, minibar, hairdrier, safe
Facilities sitting room, breakfast room, café/bar, courtyard garden, lift
Credit cards AE, DC, MC, V
Children accepted
Disabled 2 rooms specially adapted
Pets accepted
Closed never
Manager Pascal Gimel

Sixth Arrondissement

Saint-Germain-des-Prés

Grand Hôtel des Balcons

For the traveller who is searching for a budget hotel on the Left Bank, but wants to avoid one of the wackier enterprises on offer, this one may well be of interest. When you have heard about the bargain breakfast you might decide to look no further.

As its name implies, the magisterial façade of the hotel is covered in wrought-iron balconies. Inside, the reception room and large breakfast-room are dignified and gleaming, obviously well cared for by the team of maids dressed in black with white aprons. Art Nouveau is the theme, to match the fine original stained-glass windows, and there is waist-high wooden panelling with an Art Nouveau motif and light fittings in the same style; walls and ceiling are painted bright yellow. The exotic flower arrangements are the handiwork of Madame Corroyer. Upstairs, bedrooms are spruce, with ample storage space, mirrors on the walls and neat bathrooms. Brightly coloured fabrics keep the blues at bay; our inspector's room had jolly red curtains, with pretty lace ones behind, and a crisp white bedspread. As for breakfast: you can have bacon, egg and sausage, plus ham, fruit, cheese and more for the same price you pay for a couple of croissants everywhere else.

Nearby Saint-Sulpice; Jardin du Luxembourg; Latin Quarter.

3 rue Casimir-Delavigne, 75006 Paris
Tel (01) 46 34 78 50
Fax (01) 46 34 06 27
Location in a short street between Place de l'Odéon and rue Monsieur le Prince; **parking** rue de l'Ecole de Médecine; **metro** Odéon
Meals breakfast
Prices 500-800F; standard double 600F; breakfast 55F
Rooms 55; 35 double, twin and triple, 23 with bath, 12 with shower; 20 single, 15 with bath, 5 with shower; all rooms have phone, TV
Facilities sitting area, breakfast-room, lift
Credit cards MC, V
Children accepted
Disabled 2 rooms on ground floor
Pets accepted
Closed never
Proprietors M. and Mme Corroyer

Sixth Arrondissement

Saint-Germain-des-Prés

Hôtel Buci Latin

Trendy hotels, however small, don't always make charming ones; character is often obliterated by the unrelenting quest to be hip, and what seems at first stylishly minimalist turns out to be sterile and dull. The Buci Latin, however, has enough characterful touches to give it a heart. One of these is the popular basement coffee shop from where delicious smells waft up to the reception room, enlivened by a collection of American painted metal toys. Here there are sensually curving walls, across one of which are the framed photographs of the hotel's 27 bedroom doors, each painted by one of three artists. There's more crazy painting up the stairwell, the work of a New York graffitti artist: be sure to look.

We were alerted to the Buci Latin by a correspondent who enthused about the comfort of the rooms and the quality of the sheets with which the beds are simply draped (it must be said, however, that the standard of bed linen in Paris hotels is consistently high). Rooms employ terracotta and maroon colours, with *de rigueur* curvy fitted furniture, and bathrooms with prettily tiled floors. They are not large, but if you crave space, consider the suite or duplex, which with its Victorian cast-iron bath we loved.

Nearby rue de Buci street market; blvd Saint-Germain.

34 rue de Buci, 75006 Paris
Tel (01) 43 29 07 20
Fax (01) 43 29 67 44
Location just off blvd Saint-Germain; **parking** rue Mazarine; **metro** Mabillon
Meals breakfast
Prices 970-1,750F; standard double 1,150F; breakfast included
Rooms 25 double and twin, 19 with bath, 6 with shower; one junior suite; one duplex; all rooms have phone, fax/modem point, TV, air conditioning, minibar, hairdrier
Facilities sitting area, bar, coffee shop/breakfast-room, lift
Credit cards AE, DC, MC, V
Children accepted
Disabled 2 specially adapted rooms on ground floor
Pets accepted
Closed never
Manager Laurence Raymond

Sixth Arrondissement

Saint-Germain-des-Prés

Hôtel Relais Christine

Until the very recent advent of the Aubusson almost next door (see page 55), the Relais Christine was the *sixième's* most prestigious hotel. Back in the 1980s, companies took whole floors and never asked the price; in the money-conscious '90s the hotel found itself competing with less expensive establishments for the same clients. If you can afford it, though, you are unlikely to be disappointed: it has the calm, luxurious feel of a grand hotel but on a far more intimate scale; in this it is matched only by its sister hotel, the Pavillon de la Reine (see page 36).

Approached through a handsome courtyard, the Relais Christine is an oasis of dignified calm. The reception hall is coolly tiled and strewn with Persian rugs, and the ceiling retains its original painted beams. In the handsome panelled sitting-room, a help-yourself drinks table enhances the feel of a private room. Traces of the building's medieval roots are visible in the elegant stone-vaulted breakfast-room which has a huge hearth and a massive central pillar. Bedrooms are decorated with restrained luxury, with plenty of cupboard space, pretty pictures, and bathrooms in which it is a pleasure to idle away time.

Nearby blvd Saint-Germain; Ile de la Cité; Latin Quarter.

3 rue Christine, 75006 Paris
Tel (01) 40 51 60 80
Fax (01) 40 51 60 81
Location in a short quiet street between rue Dauphine and rue des Grands Augustins; **parking** free private garage; **metro** Odéon
Meals breakfast
Prices 1,750-4,000F; standard double 1,780F; breakfast 110-135F
Rooms 38 double and twin, 13 suites, all with bath (separate WC); all rooms have phone, TV, air conditioning, minibar, hairdrier, safe
Facilities sitting-room, breakfast-room, bar, meeting room, lift, garage
Credit cards AE, DC, MC, V
Children accepted
Disabled access difficult
Pets accepted
Closed never
Manager M. Monnin

Sixth Arrondissement

Saint-Germain-des-Prés/Latin Quarter

Hôtel Le Clos Médicis

The charming Pascal Beherec owns the Clos Médicis, the equally charming Olivier Méallet manages it, but it is the architect, Jean-Philippe Nuel, whose presence is most strongly felt. The new interior, from the light fittings to the wavy headboards is the outward evidence of his highly successful 1994 revamp. The ground floor is a great success, an artful mix of old and new, with split levels and curves giving a sense of style and space. A wrought-iron balustrade separates the entrance from the sunken sitting area, where a curved bar echoes the curved reception desk, and an exposed chimney with open fireplace is set between two chunks of original stone wall. With floors of wood and tile, large table lamps, elegant sofas and armchairs, the look is cool and contemporary without being characterless.

All the bedrooms have a yellow background – Monsieur Beherec's favourite colour – with different colours for the curtains and rather dull bedspreads in each room. Neither bedrooms nor bathrooms are more than adequate in size; the bathrooms are charming, though, with terracotta floors, pretty ceramic tiles and matching coloured basins.

Nearby Jardin de Luxembourg; Panthéon, Musée de Cluny.

56 rue Monsieur le Prince, 75006 Paris
Tel (01) 43 29 10 80
Fax (01) 43 54 26 90
Location between rue Vaugirard and blvd Saint-Michel; **parking** rue Soufflot; **metro** Cluny la Sorbonne, Odéon; **RER** Luxembourg
Meals breakfast
Prices 790-1,200F; standard double 886F; breakfast 60F
Rooms 38, all double and twin, all with bath, 2 with private terrace; all rooms have phone with private line, fax facility and baby listening, TV, air conditioning, minibar, hairdrier
Facilities sitting-room, bar, breakfast-room, courtyard, lift
Credit cards AE, DC, MC, V
Children accepted
Disabled one specially adapted room on ground floor
Pets accepted **Closed** never
Proprietor Pascal Beherec

Sixth Arrondissement

Saint-Germain-des-Prés/Montparnasse

Hôtel Ferrandi

Not many of the city's smaller hotels are particularly noteworthy from the exterior; the Ferrandi (and indeed its sister hotel, the Elysée, page 81) is an exception, being an immensely long and very gracious five-storey former 19thC private mansion. Indeed so long is it that all the rooms face the street.

The hotel was brought to our attention by a correspondent who had enjoyed the quiet, dignified atmosphere engendered by its elegant 18thC style of decoration. With his eyes directed firmly on the dominant white marble fireplace or the crystal chandelier, our enthusiast must have forgiven the brown swirly carpet in the *salon* (and in the sober leather-seated breakfast-room) which reminded us of an Edwardian resort hotels favoured by very old aunties. Still, old-world dignity is the key here. Bedrooms, in *toile de jouy*, display period furniture and generous beds, some canopied, with crisp white bedcovers. Rooms and bathrooms vary in size, although they are all good on storage space; the 'luxe' rooms are spacious, with room for table and chairs, and there is a rather too boldly decorated suite with ornate Venetian chandelier. No. 27 makes an excellent bedroom for one.

Nearby blvd du Montparnasse; Jardin de Luxembourg.

92 rue du Cherche-Midi, 75006 Paris
Tel (01) 42 22 97 40
Fax (01) 45 44 89 97
Location about halfway along the street, between blvd du Montparnasse and blvd Raspail; **parking** hotel garage; **metro** Vaneau, Saint-Placide
Meals breakfast
Prices 580-1,500F; standard double 800F; breakfast 60F
Rooms 42, all double and twin, 32 with bath, 9 with shower; one suite; all rooms have phone, TV, air conditioning, hairdrier
Facilities sitting-room, bar, breakfast-room, courtyard, lift
Credit cards AE, DC, MC, V
Children accepted
Disabled no special facilities
Pets accepted
Closed never
Proprietor Mme Lafond

Sixth Arrondissement

Saint-Germain-des-Près

Hôtel de Fleurie

A model hotel, rightly very popular, where charm, efficiency and up-to-date comforts go hand-in-hand. Renovated in the 1980s by the Marolleau family, who used to own the well-known Latin Quarter brasserie, Balzar, it combines an immaculate appearance (not least the pretty façade, elegantly lit at night, complete with statues in the niches) with a cosy, intimate feel. The hands-on owners – parents and two sons – are determined to keep it so, and the place always feels fresh, clean and well cared for.

Instantly eye-catching in the terracotta-tiled reception is a delightful *faience* stove picked up by Madame Marolleau in the flea market; the adjoining sitting-room, with its exposed beams and section of ancient wall, has a discreet bar and little tables covered in Provençal cloths. The basement *cave*, where a generous breakfast is served, is equally cosy, cleverly lit by uplighters.

The spotless bedrooms do not disappoint. You will find pretty billowing curtains, walls of panelled wood and grasspaper, period style furniture, inviting beds and – a rare touch – fresh flowers. Bathrooms, all in pink-hued marble, are well equipped with thick towels on heated rails and towelling bathrobes.

Nearby blvd Saint-Germain; Saint-Sulpice; Jardin de Luxembourg.

32 rue Grégoire-de-Tours, 75006 Paris
Tel (01) 53 73 70 00
Fax (01) 53 73 70 20
E-mail bonjour@hotel-de-fleurie+m.fr
Location between blvd Saint-Germain and rue des Quatres-Vents; **parking** rue de l'Ecole de Médecine; **metro** Mabillon, Odéon
Meals breakfast
Prices 680-1200F; standard double 880F; breakfast 50F
Rooms 29; 19 double and twin, 17 with bath, 2 with shower; 10 single, 5 with bath, 5 with shower; all rooms have phone, TV, fax/modem point, air conditioning, minibar, hairdrier, safe
Facilities sitting-room, bar, breakfast-room, lift
Credit cards AE, DC, MC, V
Disabled no special facilities
Pets not accepted
Closed never
Proprietors Marolleau family

Sixth Arrondissement

Saint-Germain-des-Prés

Hôtel du Globe

A gem of a hotel – tiny and quaint, with a caring team behind it. In the entrance – the building is 17thC, once part of the Abbey of Saint-Germain-des-Prés – a door set in a wrought-iron grille leads to perhaps the smallest *salon* in Paris, decorated with bird of paradise fabric on the walls and lorded over by a splendid suit of armour. Back in the hallway, a huge arrangement of flowers and a pretty *trompe l'oeil* mural cleverly reflected in a mirror, invite you to press on up the little staircase. Here on the first floor is the 'reception': simply a bureau in a cluttered private *salon*. There is no breakfast-room – breakfast is brought to you.

All the bedooms have an old-fashioned charm, with an assortment of mainly period furniture, white crochet bedspreads, and pretty canopies over some beds. No. One, for example, has stone walls, a beamed ceiling and pretty floral fabrics. In other rooms, showers and loos are tucked away behind painted folding doors. Yet though they are sweet, you might also find the bedrooms somewhat fusty, and after a couple of days our inspector reported a distinct yearning for space. Still, for the charm, location and price, he felt that the Globe was hard to beat.

Nearby blvd Saint-Germain; Saint-Sulpice; Jardin de Luxembourg.

15 rue des Quatre-Vents, 75006 Paris
Tel (01) 43 26 35 50
Fax (01) 46 33 62 69
Location in a short street which crosses rue de Tournon; **parking** Saint-Sulpice; **metro** Odéon
Meals breakfast, room service
Prices 390-550F; standard double 450F; breakfast 45F
Rooms 15, all double, 5 with bath, 9 with shower; all rooms have phone, TV
Facilities sitting area
Credit cards MC, V
Children accepted
Disabled one ground floor room
Pets accepted
Closed Aug
Proprietor Mme Ressier

Sixth Arrondissement

Saint-Germain-des-Prés

Hôtel Left Bank

If there is a downside to the Left Bank, it is the elevated prices and slightly impersonal feel that goes with its status as a Best Western hotel, despite the fact that it is run hands-on by its owner, Claude Teil. As at his three other establishments, all featured in this guide (see pages 65, 80 and 85), the hotel has a decorative theme which is carried throughout, in this case to charming effect. Downstairs there are tapestry chairs, a Persian rug, and an old stone wall adorned by a vast Aubusson tapestry. Bedrooms are delightful, with *toile de jouy* fabric on the walls, dark wood fittings, including charming old cupboard doors from Périgord, and pretty white crochet bedcovers. In the spacious triple rooms, the third bed is an elegant *bateau lit* (available for an extra 100F), much appreciated by children. Bathrooms mix dark red with pale stone coloured marble. Some of the bedrooms are exceptional for their views. No. 604 has two windows on opposite sides of the room, one giving on to the Eiffel Tower, the other across the rooftops to Notre-Dame, Sainte-Chapelle and, further away, the bulging pipes of the Pompidou Centre. Other rooms share this view, but not the Eiffel Tower as well.
Nearby blvd Saint-Germain; Latin Quarter.

9 rue de l'Ancienne Comédie, 75006 Paris
Tel (01) 43 54 01 70
Fax (01) 43 26 17 14
Location next to Le Procope, halfway along the street, which leads from Carrefour de l'Odéon; **parking** rue Mazarine; **metro** Odéon
Meals breakfast
Prices 980-1,250F; standard double 1,100F; buffet breakfast included
Rooms 31; 20 double and twin, 11 triple, all with bath; all rooms have phone, TV, air conditioning, minibar, hairdrier, safe
Facilities sitting-room, breakfast-room, lift
Credit Cards AE, DC, MC, V
Children accepted
Disabled specially adapted room on ground floor
Pets accepted
Closed never
Proprietor M. Teil

Sixth Arrondissement

Saint-Germain-des-Prés/Latin Quarter

Hôtel du Lys

For more than 50 years the Hôtel du Lys, ideally situated in a very quiet street parallel to the lively blvd Saint-Germain, has been a family-run hotel operated along *pension* lines. Nowadays it is in the hands of Marie-Helène Decharne, daughter of the original owners, and her husband. "We think of it more as a house than a hotel," she says. "Our guests are individuals; we give them a room and breakfast; after that they look after themselves, but when they are here, this is their home. Some of our clients have been returning regularly for 40 years."

In the 17thC the building was the *hôtel particulier* of loyal followers of the king, who proudly displayed the royal fleur de lys. Little has changed over the years. A venerable wooden staircase, recently restored, winds through the half-timbered stairwell to the bedrooms, all of which are individually decorated in pretty country-style fabrics. There are old wooden cupboard doors, beams, stone walls, a mixture of furniture and simple bathrooms. One room is tiny and pink, with a huge mirror behind the bed; another, next door, is just as sweet, with a jumble of beams in the ceiling. "We treat each room as if it were our own," says Mme Decharne.

Nearby blvd Saint-Germain; blvd Saint-Michel; Musée de Cluny.

23 rue Serpente, 75006 Paris
Tel (01) 43 26 97 57
Fax (01) 44 07 34 90
Location parallel to blvd Saint-Germain, between rue Mignon and rue Hautefeuille; **parking** rue de l'Ecole de Médecine; **metro** Odéon, Cluny la Sorbonne; **RER** Saint-Michel
Meals breakfast
Prices 470-600F; standard double 480F; breakfast included
Rooms 22 single, double and triple, 6 with bath, 16 with shower; all rooms have phone, TV, hairdrier
Facilities sitting/breakfast-room
Credit cards MC, V
Children accepted
Disabled not suitable (no lift)
Pets accepted
Closed never
Proprietor Mme Decharne

Sixth Arrondissement

Saint-Germain-des-Prés

Au Manoir Saint-Germain-des-Prés

Located in a prime position opposite the famous cafés, Flore and Deux Magots, this hotel has undergone dramatic transformation in the last few years. From its incarnation as the Tonic Hôtel Taranne, only the bathrooms, including Jacuzzi baths, have been retained; the rest of the hideous modern decoration has been swept away and replaced with something quite different: reproduction 18thC painted panelling, called *boiserie*, executed by craftsmen from Périgord to resemble old wood, wormholes and all. Painted in two shades of pale green, it looks charming in the public rooms, where it is complemented by Aubusson tapestries and period furniture; it particularly suits the little conservatory with leaf-painted glass roof. In the bedrooms it is mixed with *toile de jouy* fabric on the walls, and though pretty, and certainly different, its repetition makes the rooms seem uniform, even dull. Rooms are either 'standard', which means small, or large, which means fairly spacious. Most pleasant is one with steps leading down to the bathroom and a cosy attic feel; another has its own roof-top terrace. The hotel is now in the same ownership as the nearby Left Bank (see page 63).

Nearby Saint-Germain-des-Prés; Musée d'Orsay; Saint-Sulpice.

153 blvd Saint-Germain,
75006 Paris
Tel (01) 42 22 21 65
Fax (01) 45 48 22 25
Location blvd Saint-Germain at Saint-Germain-des-Prés, next to Brasserie Lipp, opposite Café Flore; **parking** rue du Dragon; **metro** Saint-Germain-des-Prés
Meals breakfast; hot and cold dishes available from outside catering company
Prices 830-1,300F; standard double 930F; breakfast included
Rooms 32 double, twin and single, all with Jacuzzi bath; all rooms have phone, TV, minibar, hairdrier, safe
Facilities sitting-room, bar, conservatory, breakfast-room, lift **Credit cards** AE, DC, MC, V **Children** accepted
Disabled no special facilities
Pets accepted
Closed never
Proprietor M. Teil

Sixth Arrondissement

Saint-Germain-des-Prés

Hôtel de Nesle

Back in the 1960s, the Nesle, tucked away down a side street, was a happening place for a generation of drop-outs who dropped in and often stayed. Then as now, no advance bookings were taken by its characterful proprietor; then as now its clients were mainly students and backpackers; then as now you were more than likely to find the receptionist lounging in front of the television.

The reception, where you also take breakfast, looks as if the owner has gone for the country cottage look, and certainly does not prepare you for what lies upstairs. The first delight, entered from the first floor, is the large lawned garden, complete with pond and palm. The next are the spotless rooms, all of which are different, but most of which display the rather child-like murals which echo each one's theme. Our inspector stayed in North African No. 4, which, exuberantly tiled, the bed draped in a simple crisp white sheet, felt fresh and clean with a charming tiled 'African shower' with lion's head water spout: you could be in Casablanca. Another, on the second floor, has a bed draped in mosquito net and a private terrace. But this is basic stuff – there are *no* extras, precious little storage space, and only one W.C. per four rooms.

Nearby Musée d'Orsay; Ile de la Cité; blvd Saint-Germain.

7 rue de Nesle, 75006 Paris
Tel (01) 43 54 62 41
Location in a little street off rue Dauphine; **parking** rue Mazarine; **metro** Odéon
Meals no
Prices 275-500F; standard double 350F;
Rooms 20; 12 double, 5 with shower, 7 with washbasin, none with W.C.; 8 single, 7 with shower, one with washbasin, none with W.C.; 4 communal W.C.s
Facilities sitting/breakfast-room, garden
Credit cards not accepted
Children accepted
Disabled not suitable (no lift)
Pets accepted
Closed never
Proprietor Mme Renée Busillet

Sixth Arrondissement

Montparnasse

Hôtel Le Sainte-Beuve

All is discretion and understatement at this essentially simple little hotel with luxurious touches: plain cream walls, restrained patterns in the rich fabrics; beds draped in white, simple furniture mixing modern designs with country antiques, attractive pictures, fresh flowers strategically placed. A log fire burns in the classically-styled *salon*, where there is also a bar.

Thanks to its owner, the Sainte-Beuve has an innate sense of style which rescues it from the rut and sets it apart, along with some pampering extra services. "We just want people to be happy," says the hotel's manager, Yves Meteigner, and so the excellent breakfast – which arrives on a tray beautifully laid with porcelain – can be ordered at any time of day or night, as well as a selection of cold dishes. During our stay we met someone who had benefited from the hotel's policy of upgrading guests, whenever possible, to a more expensive room than was booked, and another who was accompanied by her three cats – every bit as stylish as their owner – one of which had inadvertently escaped and which we found wandering down the winding staircase – a dizzying sight from the top floor – as we passed.

Nearby blvd du Montparnasse; Jardin du Luxembourg.

9 rue Sainte-Beuve, 75006 Paris
Tel (01) 45 48 20 07
Fax (01) 45 48 67 52
Location off blvd Raspail, between places Lafou and Picasso; **parking** in street or blvd Montparnasse; **metro** Notre-Dame des Champs, Vavin
Meals breakfast; room service for light meals and drinks
Prices 760-1,810F; standard double 950F; breakfast 80F
Rooms 23 double and twin, including standard, deluxe, junior suites and 2 bedroom apartments; all rooms have phone, TV, minibar, hairdrier, safe
Facilities sitting-room, bar, breakfast-room, lift
Credit cards AE, MC, V
Children accepted
Disabled access difficult
Pets accepted **Closed** never
Proprietor Bobette Compagnon

Sixth Arrondissement

Saint-Germain-des-Prés

Le Relais Saint-Germain

Irresistible, if you can afford it: a sumptuous 17thC house whose mini-lift and cramped public rooms – albeit artfully mirrored and glossily decorated – give no hint of the wonderfully spacious bedrooms upstairs. Expensive though the Relais undoubtedly is (it has just – deservedly – been awarded its fourth star), what is termed a 'standard double' here would be called a 'junior suite' elsewhere. Most 'standard' rooms in Paris give you just enough room to swing a cat. The deluxe rooms are positively enormous, with two sets of French windows overlooking the street; they are embellished with stunning antiques – mostly French country – plump sofas, lovely fabrics and well-chosen prints and pictures. One is notable for its pair of stone angels culled from a medieval chapel, another for two beautiful matching bookcases. The top floor suite is a dashing yellow, with black and white prints all over the walls, a plethora of ancient sprouting beams and a tiny sun-trap terrace.

In the morning, it's hard to choose whether to take breakfast in bed or in the adjoining café, now part of the hotel. Here you can enjoy the ambience of an authentic 1930s café once frequented by Hemingway, Picasso *et al*, married to slick hotel service.

Nearby blvd Saint-Germain; Saint-Sulpice; Latin Quarter.

9 carrefour de l'Odéon, 75006 Paris
Tel (01) 44 27 07 97
Fax (01) 46 33 45 30
Location just off blvd Saint-Germain, corner of rue Monsieur Le Prince; **parking** rue l'Ecole de Médecine; **metro** Odéon
Meals breakfast
Prices 1,290-2,050F; standard double 1,530F; breakfast included
Rooms 21 double and twin, one suite, all with bath; all rooms have phone, TV, video, fax/modem point, air conditioning, minibar, hairdrier, safe
Facilities 2 small sitting-rooms, breakfast-room/ bar, lift
Credit cards AE, DC, MC, V
Children accepted
Disabled not suitable
Pets accepted
Closed never
Proprietor Alexis Laipsker

Sixth Arrondissement

Saint-Germain-des-Prés/Montparnasse

Hotel Le Saint-Grégoire

A chic, if pricey, little hotel in a tall 18thC town house, run with affable charm by manager François de Bené. Like its sister Le Tourville (page 127), Le Saint-Grégoire was designed by interior decorator Christian Badin, but here the decoration gels – dusty pink walls, maroon carpets, floral peachy curtains, and crisp white linen bedspreads and chair covers – and a warm intimate atmosphere prevails. On wintry afternoons, an open fire blazes in the *salon*, a room dotted with antiques and knick-knacks, picked up by Madame Bouvier, the owner's wife, in flea markets and antique shops. Trellis on the walls and French windows on to a tiny enclosed garden, full of flowers and ferns, make the back part of the sitting-room feel more like a conservatory.

The colour scheme leads from the ground floor upstairs to equally attractive bedrooms, with beautiful antique chests of drawers, tables and mirrors; two bedrooms have private terraces. Bathrooms are mostly tiled in white and small, but well designed.

The ubiquitous cellar breakfast-room is a particularly pretty one, with woven floor, rush chairs and baskets decorating one wall. **Nearby** Musée Bourdelle; Jardin du Luxembourg; blvd Saint-Germain.

43 rue de l'Abbé-Grégoire, 75006 Paris
Tel (01) 45 48 23 23
Fax (01) 45 48 33 95
E-mail hotel@saintgregoire.com
Location between rue du Cherche Midi and rue de Vaugirard; **parking** rue de l'Abbé-Grégoire; **metro** Saint Placide, Rennes
Meals breakfast
Prices rooms 790-1,390F; standard double 990F; breakfast 60F
Rooms 20 double and twin, all with bath; all rooms have phone, TV, air conditioning, hairdrier
Facilities sitting-room, breakfast-room, lift
Credit cards AE, DC, MC, V
Children welcome
Disabled no special facilities
Pets accepted
Closed never
Proprietor M. Bouvier

Sixth Arrondissement

Saint-Germain-des-Prés

Hôtel Saint-Paul

The Saint-Paul, a 17thC building, was renovated in 1987. The public rooms are stylish in an unfussy way with beamed ceilings, a mixture of stone and colour-washed walls, Indian rugs, *haute epoque* and good country antiques, dark pink drapes and attractive pink and green checked armchairs. Facing the entrance, a courtyard garden is set behind a glass wall, carefully tended and full of colour year-round. The cellar breakfast-room is a particularly elegant variation on the theme, with high-backed tapestry chairs and round wooden tables. If the reception rooms have a rural feel, so do the bedrooms, all of which are differently decorated, with walls covered in grass cloth, new Sanderson's paper or enlivened with a dash of colour, and carefully lit bathrooms clad in ginger or reddish marble. Our room under the eaves felt cosy, with views over the roof tops; others have four-posters or antique brass bedsteads. All in all easy-going and well run: a pleasure to stay in. The owner's family have been talented hoteliers in France for generations; she married an Englishman, and now their friendly and capable daughter, Marianne Hawkins, is in charge, along with the hotel cat, Sputnik.

Nearby Latin Quarter; Musée de Cluny; Jardin de Luxembourg.

43 rue Monsieur Le Prince, 75006 Paris
Tel (01) 43 26 98 64
Fax (01) 46 34 58 60
Location about halfway along the street, between rue Racine and rue de Vaugirard; **parking** rue l'Ecole de Médicine, rue Soufflot **metro** Odéon
Meals breakfast
Prices 700-1,300F; standard double 800-900F; breakfast 55F-75F
Rooms 31; 26 double and twin, including suites, duplex and family rooms all with bath; 5 singles, 2 with bath, 3 with shower; all rooms have phone, TV, air conditioning, minibar, hairdrier, safe
Facilities sitting-room, breakfast-room, lift
Credit cards AE, DC, MC, V
Children accepted **Disabled** one room on ground floor
Pets accepted **Closed** never
Proprietors Hawkins family

Sixth Arrondissement

Saint-Germain-des-Prés

Hôtel des Saints-Pères

Nearly all the bedrooms in this calmly sophisticated hotel look on to a leafy, glass-sided internal courtyard where you can breakfast or take a drink in the summer sunshine. Some of the upper bedrooms also afford a romantic view across Paris toward Saint-Sulpice, whose architect, Alphonse Daniel Gittard, built this fine town mansion in 1658 as his private residence. Gittard was architect to Louis XIV and founded the Academy of Architecture; his portrait hangs behind the reception desk. A special bedroom is No. 100 (*Chambre à la fresque*), the former *salon*, where you can contemplate the vanity of 17thC France in a vast ceiling fresco of *Leda and the Swan*, either from your bed or from the luxurious *beignoir* which is separated from the bedroom only by a screen. It's now part of the Esprit de France group (see also the Mansart (page 34) and the d'Orsay (page 75).

For all this history, one might have expected rather more artfully decorated public rooms, and the sitting-room struck us as bland and business-like with its pale leather armchairs and glass-topped occasional tables. Bedrooms, however, are restful and fairly spacious, and there are good paintings on the walls.

Nearby blvd Saint-Germain; Saint-Sulpice; Jardin du Luxembourg.

65 rue des Saints-Pères, 75006 Paris
Tel (01) 45 44 50 00
Fax (01) 45 44 90 83
Location halfway along street between blvd Saint-Germain and rue de Grenelle; **parking** blvd Saint-Germain (rue de Dragon); **metro** Saint-Germain-des-Prés, Sèvres Babylone
Meals breakfast
Prices 550-1,700F; standard double 1,050F; breakfast 60F
Rooms 36; 30 double and twin with bath, 4 with shower; 2 single with shower, 3 suites; all rooms have phone, TV, minibar, hairdrier
Facilities sitting-room/bar, breakfast-room, courtyard garden, lift
Credit cards AE, MC, V
Children accepted
Disabled no special facilities
Pets not accepted
Manager Paluel Martmont

Seventh Arrondissement

Saint-Germain-des-Prés

Hôtel Duc de Saint-Simon

A stylish hotel on a stylish street, just off the boulevard Saint-Germain. First glimpsed through two pairs of French windows beyond a pretty courtyard, the interior looks wonderfully inviting; and so it is – there is a warm, beautifully furnished *salon* with the distinctly private-house feel that the Swedish proprietor seeks to maintain, and elegant yet cosy bedrooms, all individually decorated with not a jarring note. The twin bedrooms are more spacious than doubles. Everywhere you look are rich fabrics, gloriously overstuffed pieces of furniture and cleverly conceived paint effects. The kilim-lined lift is a particularly original idea.

The white-painted 19thC house backs on to an 18thC building behind, also part of the hotel, with a tiny secret garden wedged in between. Breakfasts can be had in the courtyard or in the intimate cellar bar; service is smiling and courteous. But as the hotel's own brochure points out, there are two famous cafés (the Deux Magots and the Flore) only a few yards away.

Prices are high, but not unreasonable, we felt, especially in comparison with other hotels in this category, and Gun Karin Lalisse, the manager, runs the hotel with great charm and efficiency.
Nearby Invalides; Musée d'Orsay; Musée Rodin.

14 rue de Saint-Simon, 75007 Paris
Tel (01) 44 39 20 20
reservations (01) 42 20 07 52
Fax (01) 45 48 68 25
Location between rue P. L. Courier and rue de Grenelle; **parking** blvd Raspail; **metro** Rue du Bac, Solférino
Meals breakfast, light meals
Prices rooms 1,050-1,900F; standard double 1,425F; breakfast 70F
Rooms 34; 29 double and twin, 28 with bath, one with shower; 5 suites with bath; all rooms have phone, hairdrier, safe; TV on request; some rooms have air conditioning
Facilities 2 sitting rooms, bar, lift
Credit cards AE, MC, V
Children accepted
Disabled no special facilities
Pets not accepted
Closed never
Proprietor M. Lindqvist

Seventh Arrondissement

Invalides Quarter

Hôtel Latour-Maubourg

Some of the rooms are huge (including the excellent suite) in this gracious hotel with the feel of a private house. Before the enthusiastic new owners took over in 1994, along with their three children and their dog, Faust (who will wait patiently for a piece of croissant at breakfast) it had been in the same family for 150 years. The Orsennes have wisely left well alone, upgrading where necessary, but leaving the hotel's original proportions intact. A lovely wooden staircase, with elegant balustrades, sweeps up to the bedrooms. The best of these are entered by double doors, and have marble fireplaces, French windows and period paintings. They are simply decorated, with creamy walls mixed with warmer colours for curtains and bedcovers. (You can choose between duvet or sheets and blankets; just let them know in advance.) We have had more positive reports about this hotel than any other in the guide, though our most recent inspectors thought the decoration in their room needed some updating. What emerges is the warmth of the welcome extended by Maria Orsenne. She was away during a recent visit by a couple of regular guests, who said, 'It just wasn't the same without her'.
Nearby Invalides; Musée Rodin; Musée d'Orsay; Eiffel Tower.

150 rue de Grenelle, 75007 Paris
Tel (01) 47 05 16 16
Fax (01) 47 05 16 14
Location by La Tour Maubourg metro, on the corner of blvd de La Tour Maubourg; **parking** rue de Constantine; **metro** La Tour Maubourg
Meals breakfast
Prices 550-1,500F; standard double 790F; breakfast included
Rooms 10; 7 double and twin, 6 with bath, one with shower; 2 single, one with bath, one with shower; one suite/family room; all rooms have phone, fax/modem point, TV, minibar, hairdrier
Facilities sitting/breakfast-room **Credit cards** MC, V
Children accepted
Disabled access difficult (no lift) **Pets** accepted **Closed** never **Proprietors** Victor and Maria Orsenne

Seventh Arrondissement

Saint-Germain-des-Prés

Hôtel Lenox Saint-Germain

A quiet sophistication pervades the Lenox, the more central and polished of a pair of sister hotels (see Hôtel Lenox Montparnasse, page 137). Through the entrance is a sitting area, where traditional furnishings – upholstered sofas and chairs, console tables and columns – are lightened by pale paint effects and friezes depicting classical scenes. Well-lit paintings, fresh flowers and potted plants add a touch of colour; rugs soften the granite floor. The clubby bar – all wood and tan leather seats – is open from 5pm to 2am and is currently a chic place to spend an evening, even though the drinks are pricey. Breakfast is also served here.

A total renovation of most of the bedrooms has recently been completed. As work was in progress at the time of our visit, we were unable to inspect all but a couple of bedrooms. Ones on the first floor have splendid huge windows, original cornicing and large bathrooms.

Our inspectors found the staff friendly and welcoming, making the Lenox a sound and reasonably priced choice in Saint-Germain.

Nearby Musée d'Orsay; Quai Voltaire; Louvre.

9 rue de l'Université, 75007 Paris
Tel (01) 42 96 10 95
Fax (01) 42 61 52 83
Location between rue des Saints-Pères and rue S. Bottin; **parking** rue Montalembert, blvd Saint-Germain; **metro** rue du Bac, Saint-Germain-des-Prés; **RER** Musée d'Orsay
Meals breakfast, light meals
Prices rooms 680-1,500F; standard double 740F; breakfast 45F
Rooms 34; 32 double and twin, 2 duplex suites, all with bath; all rooms have phone, TV, hairdrier
Facilities sitting area, bar, lift
Credit cards AE, DC, MC, V
Children accepted
Disabled no special facilities
Pets accepted
Closed never
Proprietor Michel Grenet

Seventh Arrondissement

Saint Germain-des-Prés

Hôtel d'Orsay

We felt a pang of nostalgia as we passed into the new Hôtel d'Orsay beneath the blue fascia with large gilt letters which announces that this was once the Solférino. The two hotels have been knocked into one, which now belongs to the same select group as the Mansart (page 34). Although the dividing wall has been demolished, the d'Orsay still feels like two separate hotels with two very different styles.

The part that was originally the Hôtel d'Orsay has been given a total makeover; bedrooms have been redecorated in pastel shades with pretty floral fabrics and attractive bathrooms in white and boldly coloured Italian tiles. These rooms are undoubtedly tasteful, comfortable and offer good value for the area, but our inspectors found themselves yearning for the big old Solférino rooms, with their scruffy blue doors and faded looks. These still exist, but look very shabby and in need of attention now. Their redecoration is planned, and in a year or so we expect all the bedrooms to conform to the new type. We were relieved to find unchanged the spring-like breakfast room with its cane chairs, glass ceiling and pale yellow walls decorated with pretty plates.
Nearby Musée d'Orsay; Tuileries; Louvre; blvd Saint-Germain.

91 rue de Lille, 75007 Paris
Tel (01) 47 05 85 54
E-mail hotel.orsay@wanadoo.fr
Fax (01) 45 55 51 16
Location in stretch of street between blvd Saint-Germain and rue de Solférino; **parking** rue du Bac; **metro** Assemblée Nationale
Meals breakfast
Prices 280-1,500F; standard double 485-700F; breakfast 50F
Rooms 50 double and twin, single, suites, all with bath or shower; all rooms have phone, TV; new rooms have minibar, hairdrier
Facilities sitting-room, breakfast-room, lift
Credit cards MC, V
Children accepted
Disabled no special facilities
Pets not accepted
Closed never
Manager David Chevalier

Seventh Arrondissement

Invalides/Eiffel Tower Quarter

Hôtel Saint Dominique

Part of the appeal of this hotel is the bubbly enthusiasm of the owner/manager Monsieur Tible, who is always ready for a friendly chat or willing to help with the most trivial of problems, and is rarely absent from his post in the delightful reception-cum-sitting-room. The heart of the hotel, this area has recently been redecorated in a cheerful yellow, forfeiting none of its former charm. A wooden spiral staircase leads from here down to a little breakfast-room – a white-painted vault with a mixture of Lloyd loom and wicker chairs – where our inspectors found breakfasts generous and attractively presented.

The small but well-equipped bedrooms (all with new carpets), and recently renovated bathrooms, are decorated in a confidently colourful style. Pretty *toile de jouy* furnishings can be seen in some rooms; in most, predominantly pine furniture, with the occasional brass bedhead.

Across a flowery courtyard, where white cast-iron tables and chairs invite summer guests to sit outside and have a drink, the annexe bedrooms tend to be smaller and more modest, but are beautifully quiet.

Nearby Invalides; Musée Rodin; Eiffel Tower.

62 rue Saint-Dominique, 75007 Paris
Tel (01) 47 05 51 44
Fax (01) 47 05 81 28
Location between rue de La-Tour-Maubourg and rue Jean Nicot; **parking** Invalides; **metro** La Tour Maubourg, Invalides; **RER** Invalides, Pont de l'Alma
Meals breakfast
Prices rooms 450-650F; standard double 540F; breakfast 40F
Rooms 34; 31 double and twin, all with bath or shower; 3 single with shower; all rooms have phone, TV, minibar; some have hairdrier, safe
Facilities sitting area, breakfast-room, garden, lift
Credit cards AE, DC, MC, V
Children accepted **Disabled** access difficult, small lift
Pets accepted **Closed** never
Proprietors Antoine Tible and Michèle Petit

Seventh Arrondissement

Saint Germain-des-Prés

Hôtel de l'Université

The mood of this dignified town-house-turned-hotel is set as soon as you step through the front door into the flag-stoned, beamed entrance, its stone walls hung with tapestries, and furnished in a masculine style, with striped velvet chairs, a grandfather clock and other dark wood antiques. The effect is rescued from being too heavy by a glimpse through glass of a tiny verdant courtyard garden.

Most of the comfortable, equally traditional bedrooms lead off grasspaper-clad corridors through velvet-padded doors. They are larger than most others we saw in this area, but not over-priced. A number have exposed beams and attractive old-fashioned wallpaper with matching bedspreads. Furniture ranges from antique wardrobes and vast carved *armoires* to small chaises-longues and velvet button chairs; ornate mirrors and handsome oil paintings – some portraits, others nautical – adorn the walls.

Guests can have breakfast in either of the two ground-floor *salons*. The one by the front door on two levels is particularly snug and private. The cellar has been converted into a conference room with an informal, rather than a corporate, air.
Nearby Musée d'Orsay; Louvre; blvd Saint-Germain.

22 rue de l'Université, 75007 Paris
Tel (01) 42 61 09 39
Fax (01) 42 60 40 84
Location between rue des Saints-Pères and rue de Beaune; **parking** rue Montalembert, blvd Saint-Germain; **metro** rue du Bac, Saint-Germain-des-Prés; **RER** Musée d'Orsay
Meals breakfast, light snacks
Prices rooms 500-1,500F; standard double 850F; breakfast 50F
Rooms 28; 20 double and twin, 6 single, 2 triple, all with bath or shower; all rooms have phone, TV, air conditioning, minibar, hairdrier, safe
Facilities 2 sitting/breakfast rooms, conference room, lift
Credit cards AE, MC, V
Children accepted **Disabled** no special facilities **Pets** not accepted **Closed** never
Proprietor Mme Bergmann

Seventh Arrondissement

Saint Germain-des-Prés

Hôtel Verneuil

Located in one of the most alluring streets in the area, this hotel, which used to be known as Hôtel Verneuil Saint-Germain, has also featured for many years in the Paris section of our Charming Small Hotel Guide to France. The subtle name change since our last edition is not the only change from new owner, Sylvie de Lattre, when she took over in 1997, although prices remain the same. The former rather kitsch decoration has been ousted and has been replaced with the traditional style of an elegant private house, much more in keeping with the building's 17thC origins.

Bedrooms, which vary in size (specify a large one), are all individually designed, some with boldly patterned wallpapers, and have antique furniture, elegant prints and pleasant lighting. The cosy sitting-room is ideal for reading or relaxing. Buffet breakfasts are taken in the stone-walled cellar, which has wooden tables and comfortable seating.

According to recent visitors, the ambience at the new-style Verneuil is happy and homely; more reports would be welcome.
Nearby Louvre; Musée d'Orsay; Ile de la Cité; Louvre; blvd Saint-Germain.

8 rue de Verneuil, 75007 Paris
Tel (01) 42 60 82 14
Fax (01) 42 61 40 38
Website http://www.france-hotel-guide.com/h75007verneuil.htm
Location between rue des Saints-Pères and rue de Beaune; **parking** rue des Saints-Pères; **metro** Saint-Germain-des Prés
Meals breakfast
Prices 650-950F; standard double 850F; buffet breakfast 50F

Rooms 26 double and twin, all with bath; all rooms have phone, TV, minibar, hairdrier, safe; some rooms have air conditioning
Facilities sitting-room, breakfast-room, lift
Credit cards AE, DC, MC, V
Children accepted
Disabled no special facilities
Pets accepted
Closed never
Proprietor Sylvie de Lattre

Eighth Arrondissement

Opéra Quarter

Hôtel de l'Arcade

Though well-placed for theatres, the opera and ritzy shops, this part of the eighth district lacks charming yet affordable hotels, so our inspector was delighted to find this one, which opened recently after a two-year renovation. The building is mid-19thC but, with the exception of the façade and some cornicing, few period details remain. Instead, a very contemporary elegance prevails. Smart glazed doors, guarded by bay trees in tubs, lead into a discreet entrance. Gérard Gallet, who remodelled the Orient Express, is responsible for the interior: colour-washed wood panelling, a striking Delisle chandelier and a happy blend of Louis XVI-style and comfortable modern furniture.

Upstairs, pastel bedrooms and bathrooms show an equally careful attention to detail, including custom-made Swiss furniture and stylish wood-framed bedheads. The linen curtains come from England, the bathroom tiles from Sardinia. Our inspector was particularly taken with the duplexes, where a staircase leads up to the small gallery bedroom. A three-star hotel with three-star prices offering four-star comfort and services. Staff are as suave and chic as the hotel itself.

Nearby Opéra Garnier; rue du Faubourg Saint-Honoré.

9 rue de l'Arcade, 75008 Paris
Tel (01) 53 30 60 00
Fax (01) 40 07 03 07
Location between rue Chaveau Lagarde and rue des Mathurins; **metro** Madeleine/St-Augustin/Havre Caumartin; **parking** pl. de la Madeleine or blvd Malesherbes
Meals breakfast
Prices 800-1,190F; standard double 1,000F; breakfast 55F
Rooms 41 double and twin, single, duplex, all with bath; all rooms have phone, TV, air conditioning, minibar, hairdrier, safe
Facilities sitting area, breakfast room, lift
Credit cards AE, MC, V
Children accepted
Disabled specially adapted rooms
Pets accepted
Closed never
Manager Dirce L. Chiesa

Eighth Arrondissement

Opéra Quarter

Hôtel Beau Manoir

One of a pair of neighbouring sister hotels, skilfully and artistically converted by their owner, Madame Teil. With an extra star than the Lido (page 85), the Beau Manoir boasts a larger reception, separate sitting-room and is generally one notch up in luxury. As the name suggests, the hotel has the look and feel of a country manor, evoked downstairs by tapestry wallhangings and upholstered furniture, stone walls, dark wood panelling and furniture, and heavy damask drapes. In the cellar breakfast-room, where a gargantuan buffet is on offer each morning, the manorial theme is continued with wooden tables and banquettes with leather seats, and an array of burnished copper pans and jugs.

Less masculine than the public rooms, the spacious bedrooms are decorated in strong sophisticated colours with every detail in place, from the carefully chosen porcelain lamps to the mellow wood furniture, specially made for the Teil family in the Massif Central. Thoughtful touches include pristine bathrobes, and duvets in every room for those who prefer them to sheets and blankets. (See also Hôtel Left Bank, page 63, and Au Manoir Saint-Germain-des-Prés, page 65)

Nearby Madeleine; Opéra Garnier; rue du Faubourg Saint-Honoré.

6 rue de l'Arcade, 75008 Paris
Tel (1) 42 66 03 07
Fax (1) 42 68 03 00
Location between blvd Haussmann and rue Faubourg Saint-Honoré, W of Madeleine; **parking** free private or place de la Madeleine; **metro** Madeleine
Meals breakfast, room service
Prices 995-1,665F; standard double 1,200F; breakfast included
Rooms 32; 29 double and twin, 3 suites, all with bath; all rooms have phone, TV, air conditioning, minibar, hairdrier, safe
Facilities sitting-room, breakfast-room, lift
Credit cards AE, DC, MC, V
Children accepted
Disabled special facilities available
Pets accepted
Closed never
Proprietor Mme Teil

Eighth Arrondissement

Champs-Elysées

Hôtel de l'Elysée

The Elysée occupies a fine building, in this case one which straddles two streets, its multi-balconied prow tapering into the corner. Sister to the Ferrandi (page 60), it employs a similar style of period decoration. We preferred the Elysée's *salon*: elegant yet cosy, with an open fire burning in the grate on cool days; in front is the breakfast area and bar, where you sit at dainty marble-topped tables. The minute lift takes you up to bedrooms which are all different and mostly quite generous on space, although sizes vary and rooms are priced accordingly. Apart from the two suites, the best rooms are on the corner, with large windows on two sides. In these you will find pretty *toile de jouy* wallpapers and canopied beds, a small table and chairs and large antique wardrobes. Bathrooms are clad in pink marble. One correspondent describes their deluxe room as 'fetching', whilst another found theirs 'rather staid and dated...not executed with much panache'. The same correspondent, however, returns regularly to the hotel having discovered the two characterful little top floor suites, which he loves, particularly the one done out in a striking yellow floral wallpaper.
Nearby Champs-Elysées; rue du Faubourg Saint-Honoré.

12 rue des Saussaies, 75008 Paris
Tel (01) 42 65 29 25
Fax (01) 42 65 64 28
Location across rue du Faubourg Saint-Honoré from Palais de l'Elysée at junction with rue Montalivet; **parking** Rond Point des Champs-Elysées; **metro** Champs-Elysées-Clemenceau, Miromesnil
Meals breakfast
Prices 660-1,500F; standard double 760-820F; breakfast 65F
Rooms 30 single, double and twin, 25 with bath, 5 with shower; 2 suites; all rooms have phone, TV, air conditioning, hairdrier
Facilities sitting-room, breakfast-room, lift
Credit cards AE, DC, MC, V
Children accepted
Disabled access difficult
Pets accepted **Closed** never
Proprietor Mme Lafond

Eighth Arrondissement

Champs-Elysées

Hôtel Elysées-Mermoz

The work of a talented designer, the effect of this recently renovated hotel is fresh, pretty and full of clever touches – like painting lemon yellow the blank walls of the internal courtyard, thereby much improving the vista from the back bedrooms.

The lobby is conservatory-style, very delicate, with marble and terracotta tiled floor, painted pale green woodwork, marbled pillars, trellis, cane furniture, a glass roof and a little yellow breakfast-room tucked behind a curtain. The bedrooms are thoughtfully designed, each with a small entrance which cuts out noise from the corridor. Rooms are either blue or yellow, with fabrics from Pierre Frey including attractive wall hangings behind the bed. Desks are cleverly slipped into a V-shaped space in the pretty panelled cupboards. Bathrooms are charming, with eye-catching sea blue basins made by a new technique using fired and glazed lava, with matching blue tiles on the floor and a large mirror on the wall above the wood-panelled bath. Suites are more luxurious, with elegant bedside lamps, rich fabrics and moiré silk on the walls. Our favourite had what looked to be Moghul Indian touches, although the charming owner assured us it was neo-Gothic.
Nearby Champs-Elysées; Grand Palais.

30 rue Jean-Mermoz, 75008 Paris
Tel (01) 42 25 75 30
Fax (01) 45 62 87 10
Location close to junction with rue Rabelais; **parking** Rond Point des Champs-Elysées; **metro** Franklin-Roosevelt
Meals breakfast
Prices 750-1,230F; standard double 810F; buffet breakfast 60F
Rooms 21 double and twin, all with bath; 5 suites; all rooms have phone, fax/modem point, TV, air conditioning, minibar, hairdrier, safe
Facilities sitting area, breakfast-room, lift
Credit cards AE, DC, MC, V
Children accepted
Disabled one suitable room
Pets accepted
Closed never
Proprietor M. Breuil

Eighth Arrondissement

Champs-Elysées

Hôtel Galileo

A breath of fresh air in this sometimes stuffy district, the tranquil, sophisticated little Galileo is Roland Buffat's most recent venture (see also Les Deux Iles, page 39, and Lutèce, page 112) and, some might argue, his most successful. Decorated in a cool combination of beige and white, and subtly lit, the bedrooms are calm and sophisticated. Most are spacious, with attractive architectural or botanical prints, wicker furniture, pristine high-tech bathrooms. Downstairs, the public rooms are also tastefully furnished, skilfully combining the traditional with the modern. So, in the congenial *salon*/entrance hall, a tapestry hangs happily alongside modern prints, antique and contemporary furniture sits felicitously side by side.

Down a pretty staircase, a small sitting area overlooks a glorious, tiny stepped garden; the trellis-framed mirror at its far end creates the illusion that it is much larger than it really is. Another cleverly placed mirror, this time decorated with pineapple lights, makes the little breakfast-room feel far from claustrophobic. Breakfast is a buffet with cereal, yogurt, eggs and freshly squeezed orange juice, as well as the usual croissants with jam.
Nearby Champs-Elysées; Arc de Triomphe.

54 rue Galilée, 75008 Paris
Tel (01) 47 20 66 06
Fax (01) 47 20 67 17
Location between rue Vernet and ave Marceau; **parking** Champs-Elysées; **metro** George V, Charles de Gaulle Etoile; **RER** Charles de Gaulle Etoile
Meals breakfast, room service
Prices rooms 800-950F; standard double 950F; breakfast 50F
Rooms 27; 23 double and twin, all with bath; 4 single, all with shower; all rooms have phone, TV, air conditioning, minibar, hairdrier
Facilities 2 sitting areas, breakfast-room, lift
Credit cards AE, MC, V
Children accepted
Disabled access possible
Pets accepted
Closed never
Proprietor Roland Buffat

Eighth Arrondissement

Champs-Elysées

Lancaster

When Swiss hotelier Emile Wolf opened the Lancaster in 1930, his housekeeper was the daughter of an antique dealer. Together they scoured Paris auction houses for furniture and *objets d'art*. More pieces were acquired during the war when guests used barter to pay their bills; a system that resulted in a splendid collection of Boris Pastoukhoff paintings. When Grace Leo-Andrieu, owner of the Montalembert (page 125), bought the Lancaster in 1996, she meticulously restored both the rooms and furniture to their former glory. The result is style that harks back to a more gracious era.

In its heyday, Wolf's hotel attracted the rich and famous, and as we went up in the red leather-lined lift, we could imagine Noel Coward enjoying the ambience. Marlene Dietrich made the Lancaster her home in Paris, and a beautiful suite, decorated in her favourite shades of lilac, is dedicated to her. We particularly liked the elegant *Salon Vert*, the tranquil courtyard garden and Oriental-style café which leads on to it. As you would expect, prices are high, but the service is so impeccable and unobtrusive that it's almost like staying in a private house.
Nearby Arc de Triomphe; Champs Elysées.

7 rue de Berri, 75008 Paris
Tel (01) 40 76 40 76
Fax (01) 40 76 40 00
E-mail pippaona@hotel-lancaster.fr
Location just N of Champs-Elysées; **metro** George V/Franklin D. Roosevelt; **parking** rue de Berri
Meals breakfast, lunch, dinner
Prices 1,650F-10,000F; standard double 2,350-2,750F; breakfast 120F
Rooms 50 single, double and twin, 10 suites, all with bath; all rooms have phone, TV, air conditioning, minibar, hairdrier, safe
Facilities 2 sitting-rooms, private dining-room, meeting room, café/bar, garden, gym, lift
Credit cards AE, DC, MC, V
Children accepted
Disabled no special facilities
Pets not accepted
Closed never
Manager Jean-Michel Desnos

Eighth Arrondissement

Opéra Quarter

Hôtel Lido

The inimitable flair of the proprietor, Madame Teil, is evident throughout this hotel, from the antique tapestries that line the walls of the reception area to the delectable homemade cakes that grace the breakfast buffet. In one of the city's quietest streets and next door to her complementary four-star, the Beau Manoir (page 80), the Lido is meticulously run, and retains a homely atmosphere, despite the immaculate decoration.

In the entrance, the heavy look of the tapestries, Persian rugs and dark upholstered furniture is relieved by light stone walls, a profusion of lamps and colourful touches – a pram full of geraniums and a tiny garden enclosed behind glass. Off comforting dark red corridors, the bedrooms are decorated in a range of exquisite fabrics, and with beautiful, specially-commissioned wooden furniture (see also Hôtel Left Bank, page 63, and Au Manoir Saint-Germain-des-Prés, page 121). Some rooms have beams and bathrooms are tiled with pretty Dutch designs. In keeping with the rest of the hotel, the cellar breakfast-room has wooden tables and red leather chairs. Breakfast is a feast of cereal, yogurt, cheese and fruit, as well as the freshly baked cakes.

Nearby Opéra Garnier; rue du Faubourg Saint-Honoré.

4 passage de la Madeleine, 75008 Paris
Tel (01) 42 66 27 37
Fax (01) 42 66 61 23
Location in tiny street off NW corner of place de la Madeleine; **parking** free private or place de la Madeleine; **metro** Madeleine
Meals breakfast, room service
Prices rooms 830-1,100F; standard double 930F; breakfast included
Rooms 32 double and twin, all with bath; all rooms have phone, TV, air conditioning, minibar, hairdrier, safe
Facilities sitting area, breakfast-room, lift
Credit cards AE, DC, MC, V
Children accepted
Disabled no special facilities
Pets accepted
Closed never
Proprietor Mme Teil

Eighth Arrondissement

Champs-Elysées

Hôtel de Vigny

This small but opulent Relais et Château hotel occupies a striking modern building with a bowed glass front, a stone's throw from the Arc de Triomphe. Inside, the style is traditional, with an abundance of mellow wood and beautiful fabrics, but not intimidating. Deep sofas and highly polished furniture fill the plush reception *salon*, where a log fire burns invitingly on chilly days. There's also a little library, perfect for tête-à-têtes, and a clubby American bar with leather tub chairs and art deco details, which is open from 7 am to 1 am and serves breakfast as well as light lunches and dinners.

Each immaculate bedroom is decorated in a different style, from the utterly feminine – floral fabrics and a draped canopy above the bed – to masculine leather combined with rich dark tones. Bathrooms blend marble and wood, and all the suites and one double room boast a Jacuzzi. The charming manager, Cécile Croisard, delights in choosing a room to suit each guest.

Our only quibbles are that the reception and corridors are lit by a harsh, unattractive orange light; and that some of the double rooms are small considering their sky-high prices.

Nearby Champs-Elysées; Arc de Triomphe.

9-11 rue Balzac, 75008 Paris
Tel (01) 40 75 04 39
Fax (01) 40 75 05 81
Location on the corner with rue de Chateaubriand; **parking** private or ave de Friedland; **metro** Charles de Gaulle Etoile, George V; **RER** Charles de Gaulle Etoile
Meals breakfast, light meals, room service
Prices 2,000-4,500F; standard double 2,300F; breakfast 100F; dinner from 250F
Rooms 37; 25 double and twin, 24 with bath, one with shower; one single with bath; 8 suites, 3 junior suites, all with bath; all rooms have phone, TV, air conditioning, minibar, hairdrier
Facilities sitting area, sitting-room, bar/restaurant, lift
Credit cards AE, DC, MC, V
Children accepted **Disabled** possible in suites **Pets** accepted **Closed** never
Manager Cécile Croisard

Ninth Arrondissement

Opéra Quarter

Hôtel Chopin

Definitely one of our top two-stars, with perhaps the most charming façade of all. It stands at the end of passage Jouffroy, one of the 19thC glass-and-steel roofed arcades which thread this no-frills shopping and theatre neighbourhood, and as we approached we worried that it would be a tourist trap. Not at all. The welcome from the receptionist was warm and friendly ("I like this job; I'm paid to smile"), and a caring hand (that of owner Philippe Bidal) was immediately in evidence in the pretty little breakfast-room, landings dressed up with a couple of chairs and a flower arrangement, and corridors clad in warm colours and lit by lights over the many pictures. Our room, No. 412, was one of the best, with coral-coloured walls and a third bed as well as simple furniture which included a desk and chairs, and a bright white bathroom. Tucked under the eaves and approached along a narrow, creaky corridor, it had the feel of an artist's garret. Set well back from the main roads, all the rooms are quiet. The continental breakfast was a cut above the average, yet reasonably priced, with hot milk for the coffee, as well as orange juice and yogurt, while downstairs a buffet is served.
Nearby Musée Grévin; Grands Boulevards; Opéra Garnier.

10 blvd Montmartre (46 passage Jouffroy), 75009 Paris
Tel (01) 47 70 58 10
Fax (01) 42 47 00 70
Location at the end of passage Jouffroy, which leads off blvd Montmartre next to Musée Grévin; **parking** rue Chauchat; **metro** rue Montmartre, Richelieu-Drouot
Meals breakfast
Prices 355-565F; standard double 490F; breakfast 38F
Rooms 36; 32 double, twin and triple, 12 with bath, 20 with shower; 4 single, one with bath, 3 with shower; all rooms have phone, TV
Facilities sitting area, breakfast-room, lift
Credit cards AE, DC, MC, V
Children accepted
Disabled access difficult
Pets accepted
Closed never
Proprietor Philippe Bidal

Ninth Arrondissement

Opéra Quarter

Hôtel des Croisés

When we first visited the des Croisés, it had been run by the same family for decades, during which time – and the key to its charm – it had remained largely unchanged. Now it has been taken over. Improvements have been made, and, thankfully, they've been done sympathetically, retaining the most striking original features. Matronly, quiet and solid, it has more the air of a provincial town hotel. The stone-fronted mansion is entered through double doors hung with café curtains. The hall is baronial, with carved stone walls and an ornate wooden archway. To the right is a pretty breakfast room, newly decorated but, with its faded pink Lloyd loom chairs, looking as it might have looked for years. The original lift, with curtained windows, takes you up to the huge bedrooms, some with extraordinary ceramic fireplaces, plaster busts, big beds, leather armchairs and – the only changes – minibars and brand-new bathrooms. Under the eaves is an apartment which we believe offers the best value in the city. For 550F a night, you get two twin bedrooms, a bathroom and kitchenette, *and* views of Montmartre. The hotel is handy for the Gare Saint-Lazare but is otherwise in a nondescript part of town.
Nearby Gare Saint-Lazare; blvd Haussmann; Opéra Garnier.

63 rue Saint-Lazare, 75009 Paris
Tel (01) 48 74 78 24
Fax (01) 49 95 04 43
Location in stretch of street between square de la Trinité and rue de la Rochefoucauld; **metro** Trinité; **parking** rue Pigalle
Meals breakfast
Prices 410-550F; standard double 460-490F; breakfast 36F
Rooms 27, 26 with bath, one with shower; all rooms have phone, TV, minibar
Facilities breakfast room, lift
Credit cards AE, MC, V
Children accepted
Disabled access difficult
Pets accepted
Closed never
Proprietor Ahmet Abut

Twelfth Arrondissement

Bastille Quarter

Hôtel le Pavillon Bastille

A 19thC townhouse set back from the busy road, whose interior has been designed with a capital D: perfect for the pair of Beautiful People who stood with us at the front door (you ring the bell and your luggage is swiftly taken for you), but a mite intimidating for the merely footsore. It's the type of interior which seems to cock a snoop, rather than to embrace and comfort. The only colours used throughout are blue and yellow, with lots of mirrors on walls and ceilings. The four tall steel uplighters in the sitting area are connected by toga-like draped material in a Classical pastiche, while those other prerequisites of Post-Modern architecture, the vertical line and the sensuous curve, are much in evidence. But if the decoration is mannered, the welcome and the service are not. Thoughtful touches include the complimentary wine served each evening in the reception room, the free soft drinks and beers from the minibar, the book of useful information in the bedroom, and the weather forecast posted up each morning. The copious buffet breakfast has a centrepiece of fresh fruit piled on ice. A small hotel with the amenities and service of a much larger one.

Nearby place de la Bastille; Opéra Paris Bastille; Gare de Lyon.

65 rue de Lyon, 75012 Paris
Tel (01) 43 43 65 65
Fax (01) 43 43 96 52
Location at Bastille end of rue de Lyon **parking** Opéra Bastille; **metro** Bastille; **RER** Gare de Lyon
Meals breakfast, room service
Prices 815-1,375F; standard double 815F; breakfast 70F
Rooms 23 double and twin, all with bath; one suite; all rooms have phone, TV (video in 3 rooms), air conditioning, minibar, hairdrier, safe
Facilities sitting area, bar, breakfast-room, courtyard, lift
Credit cards AE, DC, MC, V
Children accepted
Disabled ground floor suite
Pets accepted
Closed never
Proprietors M. & Mme Arnaud

Thirteenth Arrondissement

Gobelins Quarter

Le Vert Galant

Even if you don't stay at Le Vert Galant, try to come out here for a meal at the Auberge Etchegorry next door, owned by the same couple. In an annexe overlooking a lush lawn, the pastel Art Deco-inspired bedrooms radiate calm. Ground-floor studios boast French windows and kitchenettes. An attractive conservatory, full of plants, has tables and chairs for breakfast or coffee.

The *raison d'être* of the hotel is the restaurant. A rural inn in the early 19thC, it grew famous as the haunt of such celebrities as Victor Hugo, Béranger and Chateaubriand. Here, beside the now extinct River Bièvre, they were charmed by the voluptuous cabaret artiste, Madame Grégoire. Little appears to have changed in the *auberge*, decorated with bright copper pans and hams, sausages and garlic hanging from beams. Walls are half-panelled; the simple chairs have rush seats, the tables, crisp linen cloths. The cuisine is from the Basque region and includes such deliciously hearty specialities as duck *fois gras* and *confits*. But it is the atmosphere that makes this such an appealing place. Henri Laborde (Maité runs the hotel) is a genial host, who, even without English, makes his customers feel wonderfully welcome.
Nearby square René Le Gall; Manufacture des Gobelins.

41-43 rue Croulebarbe, 75013 Paris
Tel/Hotel (01) 44 08 83 50
Restaurant (01) 44 08 83 51
Fax (01) 44 08 83 69
Location at junction with rue des Reculettes; **parking** free private; **metro** Corvisart, place d'Italie, Les Gobelins
Meals breakfast; lunch and dinner in restaurant
Prices rooms 450-500F; standard double 500F; breakfast 40F; menus from 100F
Rooms 16; 15 double and twin, all with bath or shower; one single with shower; all rooms have phone, TV, hairdrier
Facilities breakfast/sitting-room, garden, restaurant; 5 rooms have kitchenettes
Credit cards AE, DC, MC, V
Children accepted **Disabled** one specially adapted room
Pets accepted **Closed** never
Proprietors M. and Mme Laborde

Fourteenth Arrondissement

Montparnasse

Hôtel Istria

Back in the days when Montparnasse came to prominence, the Istria counted Man Ray, Marcel Duchamp and Sati amongst its Bohemian occupants; nowadays only Man Ray's photographs on the walls recall the past, but it is still a simple, appealing – and kindly priced – place in which to stay.

The bedrooms, small but neat with pretty bedcovers and pale grasspaper on walls adorned with black and white photographs of old Montparnasse, have all been fitted out in solid elm – bed-heads, cupboards, desks, mirrors made specially for the hotel. The preponderance of wood gives the rooms a faintly Alpine air – we almost expected to see thick snow through the windows. Bathrooms (or rather shower rooms – there are only four baths) are small, but up-to-date, with pretty curved shower cubicles. Rooms on the first floor are the least expensive: they lack the grasspaper wallcovering but are otherwise the same as the rest.

Downstairs, the ground floor lobby is an attractive room mixing old with new: a Louis XIII reception desk, antique *armoire*, leather sofas, a mirrored wall, African carvings, modern paintings, soft lighting. The cellar breakfast-room is similarly cosy.
Nearby blvd du Montparnasse; Jardin du Luxembourg.

29 rue Campagne Première, 75014 Paris
Tel (01) 43 20 91 82
Fax (01) 43 22 48 45
Location in a side street between blvd du Montparnasse and blvd Raspail; **parking** blvd du Montparnasse; **metro** Raspail; **RER** Port-Royal
Meals breakfast, soft drinks available
Prices 400-500F; standard double 500F; breakfast 45F
Rooms 26 single, double and twin, 4 with bath, 22 with shower; all rooms have phone, fax/modem point, TV, hairdrier, safe
Facilities sitting area, breakfast-room, lift
Credit cards AE, DC, MC, V
Children accepted
Disabled access difficult
Pets accepted
Closed never
Manager Daniel Cretay

Sixteenth Arrondissement

Champs-Elysées

Hôtel Etoile-Maillot

Though the Etoile-Maillot adopts the same traditional and rather formal style of so many Champs-Elysées hotels, it stands out for its quiet elegance and for being, in an understated way, discernably a cut above its competitors, though no more expensive. Bedrooms are mostly spacious, with generous, deep and comfortable beds, handsome gilt and fabric bedheads, and equally handsome period wardrobes, chests of drawers and bedside tables, many of them inlaid with marquetry. Our inspector's bedroom was decorated with attractive 19thC English prints on the walls and a candelabra hanging from the ceiling. There was also room for a circular, marble topped table and a couple of leather chairs. The tiled and marble bathroom was large enough to accommodate the minibar, a much more appropriate place for it than amongst the period furniture in the bedroom. She reported a particularly restful night, and met some regular clients of the hotel who appreciated its location in this quiet, smart residential backwater west of the Arc de Triomphe, yet within easy reach of the business centres of Champs-Elysées and La Défense. The hotel is smaller than it seems – breakfast is served in your room.

Nearby Arc de Triomphe; Champs-Elysées; Bois de Boulogne.

10 rue du Bois de Boulogne, 75016
Tel (01) 45 00 42 60
Fax (01) 45 00 55 89
Location on corner of rue Duret, which runs between ave de la Grande Armée and ave Foch; **parking** ave Foch, Porte Maillot; **metro** Argentine, Porte Maillot; **RER** Neuilly Porte Maillot
Meals breakfast
Prices 570-850F; standard double 730F; buffet breakfast 45F
Rooms 27 double and twin, all with bath; one suite; all rooms have phone, TV, minibar, hairdrier
Facilities sitting area, lift
Credit cards AE, DC, MC, V
Children accepted
Disabled no special facilities
Pets accepted
Closed never
Proprietor Gilles Delfau

Sixteenth Arrondissement

Champs-Elysées

Hôtel Libertel Argentine

Hotel chains rarely offer the individuality and special appeal we seek, but the Libertel chain is an exception. One of the group's 28 hotels in Paris, all well-placed, the four-star Argentine is popular with business people – fax and computer modem points in every room, one non-smoking floor – but it is attractively decorated to a high standard with an unexpected intimacy.

The building is a grand stuccoed town house, on the outside of which a bas relief commemorates the time when South America's high society occupied this quiet street. Inside, the entrance is cool and refined, with its beige and white striped walls, freshly painted woodwork and white and black stone tiled floor. Having triumphed in the choice of a stunning Egyptian motif fabric for the hall furniture, the decorator got carried away in the bar/sitting-room. It is partly panelled in dark wood, and mesmerizing bright blue and dark pink striped fabric covers walls, curtains, sofas and chairs. Bedrooms are comfortable and smart – chintz fabrics co-ordinate with stripes and checks, lamps and prints reveal an architectural theme; bathrooms are done up in different types of marble. Staff are professional and caring.
Nearby Arc de Triomphe; Champs-Elysées.

1-3 rue d'Argentine, 75016 Paris
Tel (01) 45 02 76 76
Fax (01) 45 02 76 00
Location between ave de la Grande Armée and rue Chalgrin; **parking** ave Foch; **metro** Argentine, Charles de Gaulle Etoile; **RER** Charles de Gaulle Etoile
Meals breakfast, room service
Prices rooms 1,240-1,600F; standard double 1,300F; breakfast 75F
Rooms 40; 24 double and twin, 16 single, all with bath; all rooms have phone, TV, minibar, hairdrier, safe, fax/modem point
Facilities bar/sitting-room, 2 breakfast-rooms, lift
Credit cards AE, DC, MC, V
Children accepted
Disabled one specially equipped room
Pets accepted
Closed never
Manager M. Courtade

Sixteenth Arrondissement

Chaillot Quarter

Au Palais de Chaillot Hôtel

'The closest two-star hotel to the Eiffel Tower,' is the boast of the Palais de Chaillot, which re-opened in 1996 (after renovation) under new management. The tower is just 200m away, and though it is on a busy road, the bedrooms at the back are quiet.

A pair of charming brothers own and manage this tall thin town house, and masterminded its redecoration in a simple tasteful style. The ground floor, a sunny yellow, consists of a small reception area and breakfast-room, with ceiling fans, wicker chairs and an informal atmosphere. There is no sitting-room, and unfortunately the only terrace is on the main road at the front.

Bold maroon textured walls on the stairs lend a masculine air, reinforced by the dark red and blue checked fabric and dark wood fittings in the bedrooms. Many are unexpectedly large: the largest (and most expensive) has a walk-in cupboard. Bathrooms and showers look pristine, tiled in white and blue, and have been thoughtfully designed so that there is a space in the shower specially for your shampoo and gel. We saw few other two-stars in Paris that matched this hotel's high standard of decoration and reasonable prices.

Nearby Eiffel Tower; Trocadéro; Palais de Chaillot.

35 ave Raymond Poincaré, 75116 Paris
Tel (01) 53 70 09 09
Fax (01) 53 70 09 08
Location N of place du Trocadéro, between rue Lauriston and rue de Longchamp; **parking** rue St-Didier; **metro** Trocadéro, Victor Hugo
Meals breakfast
Prices rooms 470-620F; standard double 550F; breakfast 42F
Rooms 28; 22 double and twin, all with bath or shower, 6 single with shower; all rooms have phone, TV, hairdrier
Facilities breakfast-room, terrace, lift
Credit cards AE, DC, MC, V
Children accepted
Disabled not suitable
Pets not accepted
Closed never
Proprietors Cyrile and Thierry Pien

Sixteenth Arrondissement

Porte Maillot

L'Hôtel Pergolèse

The only hint of what lies in store behind the conventional late 19thC stone façade is in the black tubular ground-floor window supports and the blue steel automatic doors at the entrance. Inside, an expanse of immaculate wooden floor stretches away from you. Beyond reception is a sitting area with blue leather chairs, boxy glass tables and standard lamps on spindly metal stands. You could never call the Pergolèse cosy, but then that's not what it's about; it strives to be and is the epitome of designer *chic*, from the black-clad receptionist to the tower-sculpture that conceals television and minibar in every bedroom.

The designer behind the Pergolèse is Rena Dumas. Her decorative scheme is grey, contrasted with a variety of strong colours and, though pared down and functional, the bedrooms look stunning. A clever choice of warm materials includes leather tub chairs in red, blue or green, matching curtains, and beautiful ash winged bedheads. The huge beds are deeply comfortable. Just beware that you don't sever a finger on the cupboard's designer doorhandle. Bathrooms are white tiled and high-tech with stainless steel basins. As you would expect, prices are high.

Nearby Arc de Triomphe; Champs-Elysées; Palais des Congrès.

3 rue Pergolèse, 75116 Paris
Tel (01) 53 64 04 04
Fax (01) 53 64 04 40
Location between ave de la Grande Armée and ave de Malakoff; **parking** ave Foch, Porte Maillot, place Saint Ferdinand; **metro** Argentine, Porte Maillot; **RER** Neuilly Porte Maillot
Meals breakfast
Prices rooms 1,000-1,800F; standard double 1,300F; continental breakfast 70; buffet breakfast 90F
Rooms 40; 36 double and twin, 3 single and one suite, all with bath; all rooms have phone, air conditioning, TV, hairdrier, safe
Facilities sitting area, bar, breakfast-room, lift
Credit cards AE, DC, MC, V
Children accepted
Disabled no special facilities
Pets accepted
Closed never
Proprietor Edith Vidalenc

Sixteenth Arrondissement

Chaillot Quarter

Saint James Paris

If your idea of heaven is to lower black-out blinds at the flick of a switch and slide between sea-island cotton sheets, Paris's only château hotel might be the choice for you – if you can afford it. The larger, but younger sister of Pavillon de la Reine (page 36) and Relais Christine (page 58), Saint James occupies an imposing late 19thC building, in a formal walled garden where a fountain plays round the clock.

Inside, recent redecoration has done away with the previous modern, masculine style, and although everything is on a grand scale, from the balustraded staircase to the heavy panelled bedroom doors, arranged in galleries, the hotel has only 48 rooms. Appropriately the library bar has one wall devoted to bookcases, another to a bar. Leading off it, is a romantic, formal dining-room, with clouds on the ceiling.

You can work off dinner in the frightening-looking basement gym. Bedrooms are decorated in similar style to those of the sister hotels; many have striped paper and checked curtains, with feminine details such as dried flowers and prints. Bathrooms are large and luxurious.

Nearby Arc de Triomphe; Musée de la Contrefaçon.

43 ave Bugeaud, 75116 Paris
Tel (01) 44 05 81 81
Fax (01) 44 05 81 82
Location at junction with place du Chancelier Adenauer; **parking** free private
metro Porte Dauphine, Victor Hugo; **RER** Avenue Foch
Meals breakfast, lunch, dinner, room service
Prices rooms 1,750-4,200F; standard double 2,000-2,200F; breakfast 110-135F; dinner from 320F including a drink
Rooms 48 double and twin, suites and junior suites, all with bath; all rooms have phone, fax/modem point, TV, air conditioning, minibar, hairdrier, safe
Facilities sitting area, dining and meeting rooms, bar, restaurant, garden, gym, lift
Credit cards AE, DC, MC, V
Children accepted
Disabled no special facilities
Pets accepted **Closed** never
Manager Tim Goddard

Seventeenth Arrondissement

North of Etoile

Hôtel de Banville

This 1930s town house hotel offers an attractive combination of style, comfort and middle-of-the-road prices. Convenient, too, for motorists: finding your way from the Périphérique to boulevard Berthier is easy, and parking is not impossible.

The airy Art Deco building – the work of a celebrated architect, we're told – looks promising, and does not disappoint. Inside, all is tastefully decorated and comfortable, bordering on the luxurious. There is an elegantly furnished sitting area/bar, where a pianist often plays in the evenings. Another welcoming sitting-room, with antique pieces as well as comfy sofas (which can be closed off for meetings), puts the Banville comfortably ahead of the Parisian norm in this important respect.

Murals create a garden effect in the breakfast-room. The bedrooms are attractively decorated in individual styles, with thoughtfully chosen fabrics and antiques dotted throughout. Fresh flowers add a reassuring personal touch, as do such small services as having your bed turned down – a rare thing in the city nowadays. Staff are extremely friendly, and we suspect that this hotel would be far more expensive if it were on the Left Bank.

Nearby Arc de Triomphe; Champs-Elysées; Palais des Congrès.

166 blvd Berthier, 75017 Paris
Tel (01) 42 67 70 16
Fax (01) 44 40 42 77
Location on service road off blvd Berthier, between rue A. Samain and rue de Courcelles; **parking** blvd Berthier, in street and garage; **metro** Porte de Champerret; **RER** Péreire-Levallois
Meals breakfast
Prices rooms 760-1,450F; standard double 850F; breakfast 65F
Rooms 41; 39 double and twin, 36 with bath, 2 with shower; 2 triple, one family room, all with bath; all rooms have phone, TV, air conditioning, hairdrier, safe
Facilities sitting area/bar, sitting-room, dining-room, lift
Credit cards AE, MC, V
Children accepted
Disabled no special facilities
Pets accepted **Closed** never
Proprietor Mme Moreau

Seventeenth Arrondissement

Monceau Quarter

Hôtel Eber

Jean-Marc Eber remains as committed as ever to the little hotel he took over in the late 1980s after more than a decade practising his hotel-keeping in four-star Paris establishments.

The turn-of-the-century house, easily missed in a quiet residential street not far from the Champs-Elysées and near the Parc Monceau, is comfortable, well cared for and prettily furnished and decorated, and M. Eber's combination of warmth and professionalism makes sure that the hotel stays well out of the rut. The public areas are tiny, but inviting – a small beamed sitting area off the reception that also serves as a bar, and a pretty little courtyard on to which some of the bedrooms lead. Breakfast may be taken in either of these places, or in your bedroom. These vary in size and ambience, and are priced accordingly – our inspector's had a little sitting-room and a shower room as well as a bathroom. Some have lofty ceilings, others are small-scale; all are attractive, using neutral colours with elegant flower-patterned curtains. Best of all is the top-floor apartment with its own private terrace, much favoured, says Monsieur Eber, by fashion directors during Paris Fashion Week.

Nearby Arc de Triomphe; Champs-Elysées; Parc Monceau.

18 rue Léon-Jost, 75017 Paris
Tel (01) 46 22 60 70
Fax (01) 47 63 01 01
Location in street which runs parallel to stretch of rue de Courcelles between ave de Wagram and blvd de Courcelles; **parking** rue de Courcelles; **metro** Courcelles
Meals breakfast
Prices 660-1,460F; standard double 660-710F; breakfast 60F
Rooms 15 double and twin, 3 duplex; 14 rooms have bath, 4 have shower; all rooms have phone, TV, minibar, hairdrier
Facilities sitting area, bar, breakfast-room, lift
Credit cards AE, DC, MC, V
Children accepted
Disabled no special facilities
Pets not accepted
Closed never
Proprietor Jean-Marc Eber

Seventeenth Arrondissement

North of Etoile

Hôtel de Neuville

A hotel catering mainly for business clientele which we include for its animated atmosphere and the personal touch supplied by its energetic young owners. A tall white *hôtel particulier* of the 19thC covered in colourful window boxes in summer, it stands in a quiet residential square within (tourists should note) easy reach of the Péripherique and with the advantage of a private garage next door. At lunchtime, the leafy, summery basement breakfast-room becomes a popular meeting place for local residents and office workers, with a simple, inexpensive menu. The sophisticated bar and lounge – shades of fawn with blonde wood -panelled walls, and views on to a verdant, cleverly terraced courtyard garden – encourages guests to meet for drinks in the evenings, and the changing one-man exhibitions of paintings provides a talking-point.

Some bedrooms at the Neuville lack the allure of the public rooms but are fairly spacious, pleasant rather than characterful, with soft terracotta walls, brass bedsteads and chairs, curtains and bedspreads in autumn colours. One has a four poster with diaphanous hangings – definitely not for the businessmen.

Nearby Arc de Triomphe; Palais des Congrès.

3 rue Verniquet, 75017 Paris
Tel (01) 43 80 26 30
Fax (01) 43 80 38 55
Location in quiet square off blvd Pereire (Nord), between place du Maréchal Juin and place de Wagram; **parking** adjacent private garage; **metro** Pereire
Meals breakfast, lunch
Prices 590-750F; standard double 712F; buffet breakfast 55F
Rooms 28 double and twin, all with bath; all rooms have phone, TV, hairdrier
Facilities sitting-room/bar, breakfast-room, lift
Credit cards AE, DÇ, MC, V
Children accepted
Disabled no special facilities
Pets accepted
Closed never
Proprietors Pascal and Veronique Beherec

Eighteenth Arrondissement

Montmartre

Hôtel Ermitage

We were entranced when we found the Ermitage, tucked away behind Sacré-Coeur. Only a sober wall plaque announces that this is a hotel, the door opening onto a smart little gold and cream lobby, followed by a dark blue hall with deep red carpet strewn with rugs. From the reception you can see a charming kitchen with its *faience* stove from Lorraine (breakfast is prepared here and served in your room) and a little terrace beyond. Also on the ground floor: an old-fashioned parlour, with green velvet hangings, filled with antiques, photographs and ornaments. Par for the course so far, you may think, yet the Ermitage has a decorative surprise which starts in the hall and continues all the way up the stairs, on walls, doors, glass panels, skirtings. These are the charming, shadowy paint effects and murals of the artist Du Buc; the sketchy scenes of Montmartre, were done in 1986 when he was an old man.

Eclectic and friendly, with an atmosphere of calm familiarity, the Ermitage is the creation of its endearing *patronne*. Bedrooms are by and large light and spacious, newly decorated with floral wallpapers, lace curtains, large *armoires*. Bathrooms are tiny.
Nearby Sacré-Coeur; Place du Tertre.

24 rue Lamarck, 75018 Paris
Tel (01) 42 64 79 22
Fax (01) 42 64 10 33
Location at eastern end of rue Lamarck, close to Sacré-Coeur; **parking** in nearby private garage;
metro Lamarck Caulaincourt
Meals breakfast
Prices 440-730F; standard double 500F; breakfast included in price
Rooms 12; 11 double and twin, one family room; 11 rooms have bath or mini bath; all rooms have phone, hairdrier
Facilities sitting-room
Credit cards not accepted
Children accepted
Disabled 2 rooms on ground floor
Pets accepted
Closed never
Proprietor Maggie Canipel

Eighteenth Arrondissement

Montmartre

Hôtel Prima Lepic

In a bustling street, this quirky, casual hotel has an excellent location from which to explore Montmartre. Downstairs, a sitting area with white-painted wrought-iron tables and chairs becomes the breakfast-room every morning. Murals on the walls and a mass of artificial flowers and trailing vines create an out-of-doors feel. The atmosphere is airy and cheerful, and the fake flowers are charmingly kitsch rather than tacky.

Fin de siècle details are intact both downstairs, particularly in the stained glass, and in the bedrooms, some of which have wonderful high-corniced ceilings, and are all decorated in different styles. Some have been renovated in pastel colours with white furniture and a brass rail above the bed; the unrenovated – and arguably, more attractive – rooms have old-fashioned dark furniture, chintzes, and extremely basic bathrooms with baths that fill at a snail's pace, no proper shower and threadbare towels. Revamping of these bedrooms is planned; we only hope they don't spoil their character in the process. Rooms on the street side are noisy so cheaper than those at the back. Staff are pleasant, if a little breezy. Breakfasts are the minimal norm.
Nearby Moulin Rouge; Sacré-Coeur; place du Tertre.

29 rue Lepic, 75018, Paris
Tel (01) 46 06 44 64
Fax (01) 46 06 66 11
Location between rue des Abbesses and rue Constance; **parking** imp. Marie Blanche, rue Caulaincourt
metro Blanche, Abbesses
meals breakfast
Prices rooms 350-700F; standard double 380-400F; breakfast 60F
Rooms 38; 33 double, twin and triple, 5 single, all with bath or shower; all rooms have phone, TV, hairdrier
Facilities sitting and breakfast areas, lift
Credit cards MC, V
Children accepted
Disabled no special facilities
Pets accepted
Closed never
Proprietor Mme Renouf

Ile-de-France

Barbizon

Hostellerie Les Pléiades

This comfortable, down-to-earth three-star has been recommended to us by one of our readers. Set back from the main road that leads into the Fontainebleu Forest, the attractive 19thC building was once home to the artist Charles Daubigny, and as a hotel accommodated Millet, Rousseau, Ziem and other landscape painters of the Barbizon School. Nowadays the hotel combines old-fashioned charm with modern comforts such as brand-new and very luxurious bathrooms, something of a surprise in a hotel of this type. Our reader found the housekeeping 'very attentive', the atmosphere and welcome 'very friendly' and, the service 'incredibly personal, which went way beyond the call of duty.'

There is a cosy bar and a large elegant restaurant with doors on to a terrace for open-air meals in summer. Bedrooms tend to be on the small side but are light and have plenty of character. Our reader's only quibble is that 'the corridors could do with some redecoration', but goes on to praise the restaurant as 'one of the best in Barbizon – second only to the Bas Bréau (see page 144) and offers better value for money than its pricey neighbour'. In fact a double room at 370F a night seems a rare bargain to us.

Nearby Fontainebleu; Vaux-le-Vicomte; golf; riding; tennis.

21 Grande Rue, 77630 Barbizon
Tel (01) 60 66 40 25
Fax (01) 60 66 41 68
Location in Barbizon on D64, 57 km SE of Paris; car parking
Meals breakfast, lunch, dinner
Prices 320-550F; standard double 370F; breakfast 45F; menus 195-280F
Rooms 23 double and twin, one suite, 22 with bath, one with shower; all rooms have phone, TV
Facilities sitting-room, dining-room, conference room, bar, garden
Credit cards AE, DC, MC, V
Children accepted
Disabled access possible
Pets accepted
Closed never
Manager M. Karampournis

Ile-de-France

Dampierre

Auberge du Château

A traditional inn with a calm, prosperous air which stands in the centre of a stone-built country village. The building dates back to 1650 and has always been a hostelry, perhaps putting up visitors to the Duc de Luynes, an influential figure in the time of Louis XIII, whose elegant château and surrounding park lies across the road. His descendents still live there.

The layout of the auberge is a testament to its age: floors rise and descend at will and rickety wooden staircases lead to rooms; there are low-slung beams at every turn. Bedrooms are spacious and decorated in matching floral wallpapers and curtains; those at the front overlook the château and its park; at the rear, the hotel's small garden. Some have stone floors and marble-clad bathrooms. Part of the beamed dining-room reaches out to a conservatory-style extension which runs along the front of the building, opening on to a road-side terrace.

Dampierre lies in the heart of the Parc Naturel de la Haute Vallée de Chevreuse, a lovely rural area which seems very far from Paris but is in fact only half an hour away by car. There are châteaux to visit, as well as walking and pony trekking.

Nearby Versailles; Montfort l'Amaury.

1 Grande Rue, 78720 Dampierre
Tel (01) 30 47 56 56
Fax (01) 30 52 56 95
Location opposite the Château de Dampierre, 36 km SW of Paris, 16 km NE of Rambouillet; ample car parking
Meals breakfast, lunch, dinner
Prices rooms 350-600F; standard double 500F; breakfast 50F; menus from 250F
Rooms 20 double and twin, all with bath; all rooms have phone, TV
Facilities sitting-room, dining-room, terrace, garden
Credit cards AE, MC, V
Children accepted
Disabled not suitable
Pets accepted
Closed Sun eve, Mon
Manager M. Blot

Ile-de-France

Flagy

Hostellerie du Moulin

A stalwart of our Charming Small Hotel Guide to France, praised over the years by a steady flow of readers who thoroughly approve of this imaginatively converted flour mill.

The setting, with tables in the grassy garden beside the stream that still gently turns the mill wheel, is idyllic, and creates a blissfully soporific effect. Beyond the neat gardens you look out on to cultivated fields which, until the 1950s supplied the grain that was milled here. The heavy beams, wheels and pulleys of the mill dominate the cosy sitting-room, and the bedrooms, named after cereals, are as quirkily captivating as you would hope in a building of this character; space is at a premium, and low beams lead some guests to move about with a permanent stoop.

A new chef at the Moulin (reports please) specializes mainly in traditional dishes - the menu and carte have English translations, underlying the Moulin's popularity with British travellers. Claude Scheideker is a charming and friendly host who gives his little hotel, which he has been running for over twenty years, an exceptionally welcoming atmosphere. And the prices are still admirably low.

Nearby Fontainebleu (23 km); Sens cathedral (40 km).

2 rue du Moulin, 77940 Flagy
Tel (01) 60 96 67 89
Fax (01) 60 96 69 51
Location in village, 23 km SE of Fontainebleu, 10 km W of Montereau; car parking
Prices rooms 260-580F; standard double 390F; breakfast 50F; menus 150-240F
Rooms 7 double, 3 family, all with bath; all rooms have phone
Facilities dining-room, bar, sitting-room; fishing
Credit cards AE, DC, MC, V
Children accepted
Disabled access to dining-room, not to bedrooms
Pets accepted
Closed 12-24 Sep, 19 Dec-24 Jan, Sun eve and Mon (except public holidays at Easter and Whitsun; Mon evening and Tue
Proprietor Claude Scheidecker

Ile-de-France

Ermenonville

Hôtel Le Prieuré

One of our favourite discoveries, Le Prieuré is more a private house than a hotel; its owners opened its doors to guests just a few years ago, after their grown-up children had left home. For many years Monsieur Treillou worked as an engineer for the New York City Port Authority, where he learned his English. The house, an 18thC *gentilhommerie*, stands right beside the church, which shadows the attractive garden. The couple bought it as their family home 30 years ago, and Madame Treillou has filled it with the fruits of her labours as an antiques dealer. Every room is decorated in impeccable taste; only the minibars in the bedrooms break the spell. The ground floor is open to guests and breakfast is taken in the elegant parlour. The garden is English in style, with roses and fruit trees, and a little terrace; its proximity to the church makes for a calm atmosphere. Try for a room which gives onto the garden.

Peaceful Ermenonville makes an excellent base, with the forest close by, as well as Mer de Sable outdoor leisure area, and a park from the Romantic era, full of follies, which is closely associated with Jean-Jacques Rousseau, and is his final resting-place.
Nearby Fôret d'Ermenonville; Senlis; Chantilly.

Chevet de l'Eglise, 60440 Ermenonville
Tel (3) 44 54 00 44
Fax (3) 44 54 02 21
Location in Ermenonville, 40 km NE of Paris, 24 km NW of Meaux on N330; car parking
Meals breakfast
Prices 450-600F; breakfast 50F
Rooms 12 double and twin, 5 with bath, 7 with shower; all rooms have phone, TV, minibar, hairdrier
Facilities sitting-room, dining-room, garden
Credit cards MC, V
Children accepted
Disabled one bedroom on ground floor and no steps
Closed February
Proprietors M. and Mme Treillou

Ile-de-France

Provins

Hostellerie Aux Vieux Remparts

Provins is a fine medieval town, well placed for a stop between Paris and Burgundy. Like Chartres, the town, once the third largest in France, rises from fields of corn, its splendid ramparts enclosing superb medieval buildings and pretty houses whose gardens are filled with roses. The hotel, situated in the oldest quarter, the insular, carefully preserved Ville Haute, is surrounded by half-timbered buildings which give it the air of a grandiose film set. In summer the town plays host to medieval festivals and pageants when the streets are clogged with visitors, but at night: *'on n'entendait pas un chat'* – utter silence.

The Hostellerie is rather sprawling and has an emphasis on business clientele, so that the atmosphere is polished and professional rather than intimate. Public rooms are mostly in the ancient core of the building, including the refectory-style dining-room, where a rich, extensive and regularly changing menu of very French dishes is served. An excellent breakfast is served in a room beneath the eaves. Bedrooms are comfortable in a superior-Novotel kind of way. The hotel has been in the Roy family since 1858, and Monsieur Roy could not be more helpful.
Nearby Saint-Loup-de-Naud; Rampillon.

3 rue Couverte, 77160 Provins
Tel (01) 64 08 94 00
Fax (01) 60 67 77 22
Location in the Ville Haute, 90 km SE of Paris, 48 km E of Melun on N19; car parking
Meals breakfast, lunch, dinner, room service
Prices rooms 340-935F; standard double 490-650F; breakfast 55F; menus from 145F (170F at weekends)
Rooms 23 double and twin, 21 with bath, 2 with shower; 2 family with bath; all rooms have phone, TV, minibar
Facilities sitting-room, dining-room, bar, meeting rooms, terrace, garden, lift
Credit cards AE, DC, MC, V
Children accepted
Disabled 2 rooms on ground floor
Pets accepted
Closed never
Proprietor Xavier Roy

First Arrondissement

Beaubourg Quarter

Hôtel Brittanique

The hotel's smart façade is matched by the tone of the reception area and sitting room. The style here is glossy, primarily British with naval touches in the model ships and seascapes. The colours are warm, mainly red, with leather sofas and dark wood tables on which French and English language newspapers appear each morning. Breakfast, served in a small, cheery room is copious, including ham and cheese. Our inspector's verdict on her room was less enthusiastic: although comfortable (but not spacious), clean and in good decorative order, with all the normal extras, she felt let down by its banality compared to the charm and atmosphere of the public rooms - which is so often the case.

Nearby Marais; Les Halles; Notre-Dame; Pompidou Centre; Ile Saint-Louis.

■ 20 ave Victoria, 75001 Paris **Tel** (01) 42 33 74 59 **Fax** (01) 42 33 82 65 **Location** in the stretch of street parallel to quai de la Megisserie, W of place du Châtelet; **parking** Hôtel de Ville (rue de Lobau); **metro** Châtelet; **RER** Châtelet/Les Halles **Meals** breakfast, room service **Prices** 690-995F; standard double 830-870F; breakfast 58-60F **Rooms** 40; 33 double and twin, 28 with bath, 5 with shower; 7 single, 3 with bath, 4 with shower; all rooms have phone, fax/modem point, TV, minibar, hairdrier, safe **Facilities** sitting- room, breakfast-room, lift **Credit cards** AE, DC, MC, V **Children** accepted **Disabled** access difficult **Pets** not accepted **Closed** never **Proprietor** M. Danjou

Tuileries/Beaubourg Quarter

Hôtel de la Place du Louvre

Our visit was marred by an extremely flustered and unhelpful receptionist, and although we feel sure that this was just a temporary blip in an otherwise well-run establishment (under the same ownership as the Saints-Pères, Parc Saint-Séverin, d'Orsay and Mansart, on pages 71, 50, 75 and 34 respectively), we would welcome more feedback. The hotel stands right next door to the Relais du Louvre (see page 35), but being on the corner, it benefits from better views, not only of Saint-Germain-l'Auxerrois opposite, but across to the Louvre as well. Decoration is of the smart modern variety, and, we felt, rather soulless, with a ubiquitous cellar breakfast-room.

Nearby Louvre; Ile de la Cité; Samaritaine store (roof top view); Marais.

■ 21 rue des Prêtres Saint-Germain-l'Auxerrois, 75001 Paris **Tel** (01) 42 33 78 68 **Fax** (01) 42 33 09 95 **Location** in quiet side street parallel to Quai du Louvre; **parking** opposite; **metro** Pont-Neuf, Louvre-Rivoli **Meals** breakfast **Prices** 525-855F; standard double 720F; breakfast 55F **Rooms** 16 double and twin, all with bath, 4 single with shower; all rooms have phone, TV, hairdrier **Facilities** sitting area, bar, lift **Credit cards** AE, DC, MC, V **Children** accepted **Disabled** no special facilities **Pets** not accepted **Closed** never **Manager** M. Chevalier

First Arrondissement

Tuileries Quarter

Hôtel Prince Albert

We hoped when the Prince Albert changed hands in 1995, and the committed young owner, Aloum Jiwa, gave the public rooms a much-needed facelift, that he would eventually turn his attention to the dowdy bedrooms. Unfortunately the few bedrooms that have been redecorated have been done so with little taste; others look as dull as ever. A shame, since the salon with its beautiful ceiling and Egyptian *objets* is charming, and prices remain excellent for the area.

Nearby Tuileries; rue de Rivoli; Louvre; place de la Concorde.

■ 5 rue Saint-Hyacinthe, 75001 Paris **Tel** (01) 42 61 58 36 **Fax** (01) 42 60 04 06 **E-mail** aloum@aol.com **Location** between rue du Marché Saint-Honoré and rue du Sourdière, just N of rue Saint-Honoré; **parking** in street or place Marché Saint-Honoré or place Vendôme; **metro** Tuileries, Pyramides **Meals** breakfast **Prices** 430-630F; standard double 630F; breakfast 35F **Rooms** 30; 23 double and twin, 15 with bath, 8 with shower; 7 single, all with shower; all rooms have phone, TV, minibar, hairdrier, safe; 15 rooms have air conditioning **Facilities** sitting-room, breakfast-room, lift **Credit cards** AE, MC, V **Children** accepted **Disabled** access difficult **Pets** accepted **Closed** never **Proprietor** Aloum Jiwa

Tuileries Quarter

Louvre Montana (Comfort Hôtel)

A long-established hotel with the prettiest and most minuscule original lift in town, and an air of dignified dullness. We preferred the dated but comfortable and very quiet bedrooms to the made-over lobby with its ochre hues, spindly wrought-iron chairs and Egyptian motifs.

■ 12 rue Saint-Roch, 75001 Paris **Tel** (01) 42 60 35 10 **Fax** (01) 42 61 12 28 **Meals** breakfast **Prices** 780-1,090F; standard double 860F; breakfast 55F **Rooms** 25 double and twin, 22 with bath, 3 with shower; all rooms have phone, TV, minibar, iron and ironing board (most rooms), hairdrier **Credit cards** AE, DC, MC, V **Closed** never

Tuileries Quarter

Hôtel de la Tamise

Since the departure of the friendly Spanish manager, Monsieur Antonio, the Tamise has lost some of its charm for us, and its air of faded gentility seems to be a little more faded now. A mirrored entrance hall with potted plants, tessallated floor and an Edwardian feel opens on to a lovely little salon on one side and a breakfast room on the other. A tiny wrought-iron and gilt lift takes you up to fairly dull bedrooms with skimpy-looking beds.

■ 4 rue d'Alger, 75001 Paris **Tel** (01) 42 60 51 54 **Fax** (01) 42 86 89 97 **Meals** breakfast **Prices** 450-752F; standard double 712-752F; breakfast 40F **Rooms** 18; 14 double and twin with bath; 4 single with shower; all rooms have phone, TV **Credit cards** MC, V **Closed** never

Second Arrondissement

Les Halles

Grand Hôtel de Besançon

If you prefer a small hotel which is smart, spanking new and undemanding rather than characterful, then this may be a candidate. Though lacking in atmosphere, it has other points in its favour, not least the reasonable prices and the location: pedestrianized rue Montorgeuil, lined with colourful flower and vegetable stalls, is the only street in Les Halles to retain the area's former market status. A long mirrored entrance hall and stairs lead to the reception. Bedrooms are fairly spacious, with wooden fittings, reproduction Louis Philippe furniture and prints of old masters; bathrooms are bright white, each with a pretty tiled border. Dull breakfast area – best to take it in your room.
Nearby Saint-Eustache; Forum des Halles; Pompidou Centre.

■ 56 rue Montorgueil, 75002 Paris **Tel** (01) 42 36 41 08 **Fax** (01) 45 08 08 79 **Location** in pedestrianized street between rue Etienne Marcel and rue Réamur; **parking** rue Saint-Denis; **metro** Etienne Marcel, Les Halles; **RER** Châtelet/Les Halles **Meals** breakfast **Prices** 550-760F; standard double 680F; breakfast 40F **Rooms** 20; 18 double and twin, all with bath; 2 single, both with shower; all rooms have phone, TV, hairdrier **Facilities** breakfast-room, lift **Credit cards** AE, DC, MC, V **Children** accepted **Disabled** access difficult **Pets** not accepted **Closed** never **Proprietor** M. Boudaa

Opéra Quarter

Hôtel Gaillon Opéra

There is a rustic feel about this busy hotel in the heart of the Right Bank shopping district, especially the beamed and stone-walled lobby. Many of the bedrooms are also beamed, with country-style furnishings, but they are neither light nor spacious. Some bathrooms have been renovated recently; reports please.

■ 9 rue Gaillon, 75002 Paris **Tel** (01) 47 42 47 74 **Fax** (01) 47 42 01 23 **Meals** breakfast **Prices** 600-1,450F; standard double 650-1,050F; breakfast 40F **Rooms** 19 double and twin, 7 single, all with bath; all rooms have phone, fax/modem point, TV, air conditioning (in half), hairdrier, safe **Credit cards** AE, DC, MC, V **Closed** never

Opéra Quarter

Le Stendhal

Strictly for expense account clients with little interest in value for money, Le Stendhal is wickedly expensive, especially when compared to the much more spacious and gracious Mansart across the road (see page 34). The hotel is handsomely decorated, though without much originality (save the terrific basins); public areas are cramped.

■ 22 rue Danielle Casanova, 75002 Paris **Tel** (01) 44 58 52 52 **Fax** (01) 44 58 52 00 **Meals** breakfast **Prices** 1,440F-2,000F; standard double 1,630F; breakfast 100F **Rooms** 17 double and twin, 3 suites, all with bath; all rooms have phone, fax/modem point/private line, TV, air conditioning, minibar, hairdrier, safe **Credit cards** AE, DC, MC, V **Closed** never

Fourth Arrondissement

Beaubourg Quarter/Marais

Hôtel Beaubourg

Just round the corner from the Pompidou Centre, this is a straightforward hotel in a converted 17thC building. Although the interior verges on the bland, there are enough attractive touches to keep up one's interest, and we had a warm welcome, a comfortable night and a modest bill at the end. First impressions are favourable, with the beamed reception/sitting area and the wide corridor beyond enormously enhanced by the use of a warm, deep red wallcovering; a pair of pretty armchairs and soft lighting add to the welcoming feel. There is also a stone-vaulted cave breakfast-room, plainly furnished, and a little courtyard garden, full of trailing plants, over which some of the bedrooms look. These rooms are very quiet – opt for one if you can, or the room on the ground floor with its own terrace.
Nearby Pompidou Centre; Les Halles; Marais; Notre Dame.

■ 11 rue Simon Lefranc, 75004 Paris **Tel** (01) 42 74 34 24 **Fax** (01) 42 78 68 11 Location in side street off rue du Renard, opposite Pompidou Centre; **parking** Pompidou Centre; **metro** Rambuteau; **RER** Châtelet/Les Halles **Meals** breakfast **Prices** 490-690F; standard double 590F; breakfast 40F **Rooms** 28 double and twin; 24 with bath, 4 with shower; all rooms have phone, TV, minibar, hairdrier Facilities sitting area, breakfast room, courtyard, lift **Credit card**s AE, DC, MC, V **Children** accepted **Disabled** one room on ground floor **Pets** accepted **Closed** never **Proprietor** Mme Morand

Marais

Grand Hôtel Jeanne d'Arc

In contradiction to its name, this is a modest two-star hotel, fiercely popular with Americans, attracted by the 17thC building and unbeatable prices for the area. Downstairs the decoration tends to be eclectic: witness the extraordinary 'fantasy' tiled mirror, which assaults you visually as you enter. Commissioned to embody the Joan of Arc theme, the frame is made of mosaic tiles and emblazoned with zinc *fleur de lys*, flags, coloured glass studs and an army of flashing candle lights. The breakfast-room has wooden tables and chairs and sponged walls in a peachy colour with a frieze of painted trees. Clouds and stars are incorporated into the scheme of the tiny back sitting-room. Decoration in the simple bedrooms is fresh and less ambitious, though furniture is uninspired. Attic rooms afford great views. Bathrooms are spacious, some with startling blue splash effect tiles.
Nearby place des Vosges; Musée Carnavalet; Musée Picasso.

■ 3 rue de Jarente, 75004 Paris **Tel** (01) 48 87 62 11 **Fax** (01) 48 87 37 31; **parking** rue Saint-Antoine; **metro** Saint Paul, Bastille **Meals** breakfast **Prices** rooms 300-600F; standard double 425F; breakfast 35F **Rooms** 36; 24 double and twin, 12 family, all with bath or shower; all rooms have phone, TV **Facilities** sitting-room, breakfast-room, lift **Credit cards** MC, V **Children** accepted **Disabled** some rooms on ground floor **Closed** never **Proprietor** Mme Mesenge

Fourth Arrondissement

Marais

Hôtel de la Place des Vosges

Set in a quiet street only 25 metres from one of the loveliest squares in Paris (but please note that, despite its name, it is not *in* the place des Vosges), this simple 17thC house is entirely in harmony with the surrounding area. The *salon* is suitably traditional and rustic in style; bedrooms have less character (what's new?) with basic furnishings and fittings and many are very small. The family room has two extra beds, and several others have one extra bed which acts as a couch if you don't need it. The lift could be the world's smallest. There is a certain homely charm about the place, and if you're on a budget but want a great location, this is a good bet. Old Monsieur Cros does not speak English; his son, young Monsieur Cros speaks a little.
Nearby Musée Carnavalet; Musée Picasso; Ile Saint-Louis.

■ 12 rue de Birague, 75004 Paris **Tel** (01) 42 72 60 46 **Fax** (01) 42 72 02 64 **Location** in short street off rue Saint-Antoine leading to place des Vosges; **parking** rue Saint-Antoine; **metro** Saint-Paul **Meals** breakfast **Prices** 365-610F; standard double 545-560F, breakfast included **Rooms** 16, 11 with bath, 5 with shower; all rooms have phone, TV, hairdrier **Facilities** sitting area, breakfast-room, lift **Credit cards** AE, DC, MC, V **Children** accepted **Disabled** not suitable **Pets** accepted **Closed** never **Proprietor** M. Cros

Marais

Hôtel du Septième Art

Not just a hotel, but a bar, gallery, shop and hotel rolled into one. From the outside, it looks like a typical Marais shopfront, its windows filled with a wonderfully eccentric mix of miniature figures, representing famous film stars and jazz musicians, and gleaming *espresso* machines. Inside, through a mirror-tiled entrance, is a cosy beamed bar with ceiling fans and potted palms, navy velvet banquettes, café chairs, marble-topped tables, a real fire, and the reason behind its name – framed posters for old movies, everywhere. The posters, figures and coffee machines are all for sale. The bar is open until midnight and for breakfast. Bedrooms are simple and unexceptional, but the attic room has plenty of space. The ambience is matched by the friendly staff.
Nearby place des Vosges; Musée Carnavalet; Hôtel de Ville.

■ 20 rue Saint-Paul, 75004 Paris **Tel** (01) 44 54 85 00 **Fax** (01) 42 77 69 10 **Location** between rue Charles V and rue Neuve Saint-Pierre; **parking** rue Saint-Antoine; **metro** Saint Paul, Pont Marie, Sully Morland **Meals** breakfast **Prices** rooms 295-670F; standard double 420-490F; breakfast 45F **Rooms** 23; 22 double and twin, all with bath or shower; one single without shower or WC; all rooms have phone, TV, safe **Facilities** bar/breakfast-room, cellar meeting room **Credit cards** AE, DC, MC, V **Children** accepted **Disabled** access difficult (no lift) **Pets** accepted **Closed** never **Manager** M. Michel

Fourth Arrondissement

Ile de la Cité

Hospitel

Go past radiology, opthalmology and geriatrics, then up to the top floor of the Hôtel-Dieu hospital to find a hotel mainly patronized by patients and their families, but by budget-conscious (and hypochondriac?) tourists too. Bright, comfortable rooms, some with cathedral views.

■ Hôtel-Dieu, 1 place du Parvis Nôtre-Dame, 75004 Paris **Tel** (01) 44 32 01 00 **Fax** (01) 44 32 01 16 **Meals** breakfast **Prices** 480-550F; standard double 550F; breakfast 40F **Rooms** 14, all with bath; all rooms have phone, TV **Credit cards** not accepted **Closed** never

Ile Saint-Louis

Hôtel de Lutèce

Sister hotel to the Deux Iles (see page 39); same feel, same price, but neither lobby nor bedrooms are as appealing: the latter, decorated in Indian prints, somehow feel a bit bleak, and while bathrooms are larger, they lack the Deux Iles' pretty ceramics.

■ 59 rue Saint-Louis-en-l'Ile, 75004 Paris **Tel** (01) 43 26 23 52 **Fax** (01) 43 29 60 25 **Meals** breakfast **Prices** 700-870F; standard double 840F; breakfast 50F **Rooms** 20 double and twin, 1 single, 2 family, all with bath or shower; all rooms have phone, TV, air conditioning, hairdrier, safe **Credit cards** AE, V, MC **Closed** never

Marais

Grand Hôtel Malher

Run by owner, Didier Fossiez, who loves his role of genial host, divulging secret short-cuts to his guests. Decoration is simple: marble-tiled entrance with leather furniture; bedrooms all a trifle bland – floral fabric, velvet chairs, innocuous prints.

■ 5 rue Malher, 75004 Paris **Tel** (01) 42 72 60 92 **Fax** (01) 42 72 25 37 **Meals** breakfast **Prices** rooms 490-990F; standard double 590-690F; breakfast 47F **Rooms** 31; 30 double and twin, 1 triple, all with bath or shower, phone, TV, minibar, hairdrier **Credit cards** AE, MC, V **Closed** never

Marais

Hôtel Saint-Paul-Le-Marais

Newish hotel with a stylish modern lobby dominated by large-black leather armchairs, and with an attractive curved bar in the corner. Double-glazed bedrooms are bland, enlivened by the odd splash of colour on the walls here and there. Mini-suites have staircases up to a third bed, which a child might enjoy.

■ 8 rue de Sévigné, 75004 Paris **Tel** (01) 48 04 97 27 **Fax** (01) 48 87 37 04 **Meals** breakfast **Prices** 550-1,700F; standard double 650-750F; breakfast 60F **Rooms** 15 double and twin, 4 mini-suites, all with bath; 8 single with shower; all rooms have phone, TV, hairdrier, safe **Credit cards** AE, DC, MC, V **Closed** never

Fifth Arrondissement

Latin Quarter

Hôtel Esmeralda

A hotel of great character, loved by legions of faithful guests as much for its charmingly eccentric owner as for its genuine Left Bank atmosphere and superb position. Yet sadly, devoted as we have been to the Esmeralda – it has featured in our *Charming Small Hotel Guide to France* for many years – it does now appear to be in gentle decline: witness the star which has been crudely whitewashed out on the tourist board plaque outside the hotel, testament to its demotion from a two- to a one-star establishment; and the rooms, with their old beams, stone walls, quarry tile floors and carefree assortment of furniture and fabrics, which are shabby, creaky, not very clean and hard to recommend, at least not to newcomers; devotees will make their own choice. Prices have not changed for three years.
Nearby Notre-Dame; Sainte-Chapelle; Musée de Cluny; Ile Saint-Louis.

■ 4 rue Saint-Julien-le-Pauvre, 75005 Paris **Tel** (01) 43 54 19 20 **Fax** (01) 40 51 00 68 **Location** in side street off quai de Montebello, opposite a little public garden; **parking** place Maubert; **metro** Saint-Michel; **RER** Saint-Michel **Meals** breakfast **Prices** 160-600F; standard double 490F; breakfast 40F **Rooms** 20 double and twin, with bath, shower or washbasin; all rooms have phone **Facilities** breakfast-room, sitting area **Credit cards** not accepted **Children** accepted **Disabled** not suitable (no lift) **Pets** accepted **Closed** never **Proprietor** Mme Bruel

Latin Quarter

Hôtel Résidence Henri IV

If you are looking for somewhere to stay where you can do some limited self-catering, you might consider this hotel, set at the end of a quiet cul-de-sac. Each room contains a minute kitchenette, consisting of hob, microwave, fridge and storage space which can be hidden away behind a pull-down screen. The apartments have a large comfortable sofa bed in the sitting-room, so that a family of four could fit in. The rooms are rather blandly decorated, without much style, which is a pity because they have splendid period features, with ornate ceilings and panelled walls. Some retain marble fireplaces and pretty painted plaster figures on the walls. Staff are helpful and friendly.
Nearby Panthéon; Musée de Cluny; Notre-Dame; Sainte-Chapelle.

■ 50 rue des Bernadins, 75005 Paris **Tel** (01) 44 41 31 81 **Fax** (01) 46 33 93 22 **Location** at the end of street, in the section between rue Monge and rue des Ecoles; **parking** place Maubert; **metro** Maubert Mutualité; **RER** Saint-Michel **Meals** breakfast **Prices** 900-1,400F; standard double 900F; breakfast 40F **Rooms** 12; 6 apartments, 5 double, one single, all with bath; all rooms have kitchenette, phone, fax/modem point, TV, minibar, hairdrier, safe **Facilities** breakfast-room, sitting area, lift **Credit cards** AE, DC, MC, V **Children** accepted **Disabled** one room on ground floor **Pets** not accepted **Closed** never **Owner** Corinne Brethous

Fifth Arrondissement

Latin Quarter

Hôtel de Notre-Dame

The hotel's frontage has large plate glass windows with attractive views down the street towards the *quai*, while the smart reception room has a marble floor, stone walls and a mixture of old and new furniture. We found the reception staff helpful and friendly. Bedrooms have been renovated recently. Some have a Japanese-style partition between bedroom and bathroom. They are however very quiet, especially those which look on to an internal courtyard rather than the street – although the street-facing rooms are larger, with French windows opening on to pretty window boxes.

Nearby Musée de Cluny; Notre-Dame; Ile Saint-Louis.

■ 19 rue Maître Albert, 75005 Paris **Tel** (01) 43 26 79 00 **Fax** (01) 46 33 50 11 **Location** near rue Lagrange end of street; **parking** rue Lagrange; **metro** Saint Michel Notre-Dame; Maubert-Mutualité; **RER** Saint-Michel **Meals** breakfast **Prices** 750-850F; standard double 820F; breakfast 40F **Rooms** 34 double and twin, 33 with bath, one with shower; all rooms have phone, TV, minibar, hairdrier, safe **Facilities** sitting area, breakfast-room, lift **Credit cards** AE, DC, MC, V **Children** accepted **Disabled** access difficult **Pets** not accepted **Closed** never **Proprietor** M. Fouhety

Latin Quarter

Hôtel des Trois Collèges

In the university heartland, this hotel has a historically important location on the site of the crossroads at the centre of the ancient Roman town; maps verifying this cover the walls. In the pretty glass-roofed salon, among Lloyd loom chairs, ancient pots are on display - finds from archaeological digs here. Even the original well is visible in a corner. Its real attraction is the simple *salon de thé* next door, an integral part of the hotel. Popular with students, teachers and tourists alike, the quiches, salads and delectable pastries, as well as the simple decoration – white walls, blue and natural wood furniture – make it an agreeable place to meet. The bedrooms, with their white formica and wood fixtures, are, however, pedestrian. Staff are friendly and attentive.

Nearby Panthéon; Sorbonne; blvd Saint-Michel; Musée de Cluny.

■ 16 rue Cujas, 75005 Paris **Tel** (01) 43 54 67 30 **Fax** (01) 46 34 02 99 **Location** between rue V. Cousin and blvd Saint-Michel; **parking** rue Soufflot; **metro** Luxembourg; **RER** Luxembourg **Meals** breakfast, light meals **Prices** rooms 380-650F; standard double 540F; breakfast 42F **Rooms** 44; 36 double and twin, 2 triple, all with bath or shower; 6 single with shower; all rooms have phone, TV, hairdrier **Facilities** sitting-room, *salon de thé*, lift **Credit cards** AE, DC, MC, V **Children** accepted **Disabled** no special facilities **Pets** accepted **Closed** never **Proprietors** M. and Mme Wyplosz

Fifth Arrondissement

Latin Quarter

Hôtel Cluny Sorbonne

A straightforward budget hotel, included for its excellent location, its clean appearance, airy, summer-yellow lobby and value-for-money family room – a light top-floor room with desk and two double beds covered in pretty white bedspreads.

■ 8 rue Victor Cousin, 75005 Paris **Tel** (01) 43 54 66 66 **Fax** (01) 43 29 68 07 **Meals** breakfast **Prices** 380-700F; standard double 420-430F; breakfast 37F **Rooms** 23 double and twin, one family, all with bath; all rooms have phone, TV **Credit cards** AE, MC, V **Closed** never

Latin Quarter

Libertel Quartier Latin

A 'library' hotel in the heart of the Latin Quarter. It's part of the Libertel chain, though, and too self-conscious to be really successful. The entrance is dominated by a wall of bookcases. A Baudelaire quote is etched in a frieze; upstairs lines from Proust adorn the carpets. Bedrooms are modern and comfortable.

■ 9 rue des Ecoles, 75005 Paris **Tel** (01) 44 27 06 45 **Fax** (01) 43 25 36 70 **Meals** breakfast **Prices** 910-1,050F; standard double 975F; breakfast 75F **Rooms** 29 single, double and twin, junior suites, all with bath; all rooms have phone, TV, air conditioning, minibar, tea/coffee kit, hairdrier, safe **Credit cards** AE, DC, MC, V **Closed** never

Latin Quarter

Hôtel du Panthéon

The best thing about this hotel is its position – right opposite the Panthéon. The view is one of the city's greats, particularly at night. A comfortable 18thC mansion with pastel decoration, this is a solid, dependable place which holds no surprises – neither frightful nor delightful. Bedrooms are pedestrian, staff helpful.

■ 19 place du Panthéon, 75005 Paris **Tel** (01) 43 54 32 95 **Fax** (01) 43 26 64 65 **Meals** breakfast **Prices** 750-1,000F; standard double 900F; breakfast 50F **Rooms** 35; 34 double and twin, one single, all with bath; all rooms have phone, TV, air conditioning, minibar, hairdrier **Credit cards** AE, DC, MC, V **Closed** never

Gobelins/Luxembourg Quarter

Port-Royal-Hôtel

A family-run one-star hotel – no frills, but spotlessly clean and great value. It has a cosy salon, breakfast-room and simple bedrooms (some with new bathrooms), unfortunately displaying too much plastic. There is a tiny garden where you can sit out.

■ 8 blvd de Port Royal, 75005 Paris **Tel** (01) 43 31 70 06 **Fax** (01) 43 31 33 67 **Meals** breakfast **Prices** rooms 272-444F; standard double 444F; breakfast 27F **Rooms** 45; 35 double and twin, 18 with bath or shower; all rooms have phone **Credit cards** not accepted **Closed** never

Sixth Arrondissement

Montparnasse

L'Atelier Montparnasse Hôtel

A tiny hotel whose engaging, arty atmosphere, engendered by its owner, Marie-José Tible, reflects something of the laid-back, artistic legacy of the area. The '30s style ground floor has a magnificent mosaic floor, the walls hung with the paintings of the young artists whom Marie-José champions (she holds regular one-man shows). The smallish bedrooms (there are two large ones on the top floor) are notable for their highly original mosaic bathrooms, each mosaic – executed by the mother of the previous owner – representing a famous modern painting, by Modigliani, Gaugin, Foujita and others. Bedrooms have all been redecorated, which highlights how desperately some of the mosaics are in need of repair. A daunting task.
Nearby blvd du Monparnasse; Jardin du Luxembourg; blvd Saint-Germain.

■ 49 rue Vavin, 75006 Paris **Tel** (01) 46 33 60 00 **Fax** (01) 40 51 04 21 **Location** in stretch of street between blvd Montparnasse and blvd Raspail; **parking** in street or blvd Montparnasse; **metro** Vavin **Meals** breakfast **Prices** 700-1,100F; standard double 820F; breakfast 50F **Rooms** 17, all double and twin, all with bath; all rooms have phone, TV, minibar, hairdrier **Facilities** sitting-room, breakfast-room, lift **Credit cards** AE, DC, MC, V **Children** accepted **Disabled** no special facilities **Pets** accepted **Closed** never **Proprietor** Marie-José Tible

Montparnasse

Hôtel Danemark

Everything about this smart hotel is deliberately stylish: the triple-arched, electric-blue frontage, the striking modern art, the shiny chairs, low glass tables, slick black, green and blue furniture and stylish wall and table lights. That at least describes the ground floor reception area; the bedrooms were, to our mind, less impressive. Although a previous inspector had found them 'refreshingly simple', and they are plainly meant to be stylish in a clean, modern way, we felt that they were rather insipid, with bland curtains and bedcovers and 'off the peg' cupboards and headboards. New bathrooms are planned. Each floor has its own colour scheme: we like the fourth floor best – blue with a pretty motif. Friendly, helpful staff. More reports please.
Nearby blvd du Montparnasse; blvd Saint-Germain; Jardin du Luxembourg.

■ 21 rue Vavin, 75006 Paris **Tel** (01) 43 26 93 78 **Fax** (01) 46 34 66 06 **Location** between blvd Raspail and rue Notre-Dame de Champs; **parking** in street or blvd Montparnasse; **metro** Vavin **Meals** breakfast **Prices** 620-790F; standard double 690F; breakfast 55F **Rooms** 15, all double and twin, 14 with bath, one with jacuzzi; all rooms have phone, TV, minibar, hairdrier **Facilities** sitting-room, breakfast-room, lift **Credit cards** AE, DC, MC, V **Children** accepted **Disabled** no special facilities **Pets** accepted **Closed** never **Proprietor** Jean Nurit

Sixth Arrondissement

Saint-Germain-des-Prés

L'Hôtel

For many years Guy Louis Dubucheron's L'Hôtel was *the* place to stay on the Left Bank – wildly ornate, showbizzy, exclusive. But times changed, and we started to receive too many complaints from readers (bathroom too small to dry in, no hot water, scant apology, disengaged staff, hot and stuffy, sub-standard breakfast, all at hugely inflated prices). A recent visit coincided with a change of management. Our inspector found the lovely domed stairwell still impressive, but the decoration, with its preponderance of velvet and leopard skin wallcoverings, dated and tired in places. She was moved when she stood in the famous room in which Oscar Wilde died beyond his means, but was heartily glad she didn't have to sleep in it. Reports please.

Nearby Musée d'Orsay; blvd Saint-Germain; Louvre; Saint-Chapelle; Notre-Dame.

■ 13 rue des Beaux-Arts, 75006 Paris **Tel** (01) 43 25 27 22 **Fax** (01) 43 25 64 81 **Location** in short street between rue de Seine and rue Bonaparte; **parking** rue Mazarine; **metro** Saint-Germain-des-Prés **Meals** breakfast; room service **Prices** 800-4,000F; standard double 1,800-2,800F; breakfast 110F **Rooms** 25 double and twin, 15 with bath, 10 with shower; 2 apartments; all rooms have phone, TV, air conditioning, minibar, hairdrier, safe **Facilities** sitting-room, breakfast-room, bar, lift **Credit cards** AE, DC, MC, V **Children** accepted **Disabled** no special facilities **Pets** accepted **Closed** never **Manager** M. Besnard

Saint-Germain-des-Prés

Hôtel Louis II

A hotel which has faded charm, though we felt, at the time of our visit, that it had faded rather too far. Housed in a pretty 18thC building, it boasts almost as many exposed beams as the Jeu de Paume (see page 40), but here they are married with lace bedspreads and tablecloths, heavy gilt mirrors, brocade-covered chairs and solid antique furniture. The sitting-room has huge windows and, though filled with tables and chairs, feels spacious. It doubles as a breakfast-room each morning. Upstairs, the sloping floors are charming, but the scruffy corridors are not. The most desirable, if eccentrically shaped, bedrooms are under the eaves. Bathrooms and showers are antique. A new owner has taken over the Louis II; reports please.

Nearby blvd Saint-Germain; Jardin du Luxembourg; Ile de la Cité.

■ 2 rue Saint-Sulpice, 75006 Paris **Tel** (01) 46 33 13 80 **Fax** (01) 46 33 17 29 **Location** on corner with rue de Condé; **parking** place Saint-Sulpice; **metro** Odéon, Mabillon **meals** breakfast **Prices** rooms 555-980F; standard double 580-645F; breakfast 52F **Rooms** 22; 20 double and twin, 2 triple, all with bath or shower; all rooms have phone, TV, minibar, hairdrier, safe **Facilities** sitting/breakfast-room, lift **Credit cards** AE, DC, MC, V **Children** accepted **Disabled** no special facilities **Pets** accepted **Closed** never **Proprietor** M Meynant

Sixth Arrondissement

Saint-Germain-des-Prés

Hôtel des Marronniers

The allure of the Marronniers lies in its situation, tucked away from the bustle of Saint-Germain between a quiet courtyard in front and a lovely garden behind. The ground floor particularly has the feel of a country hotel, its flowery conservatory – Empire-style curtains, white wrought-iron furniture – opening on to the garden beyond. In the contrastingly dark basement, stone vaulted cellars form a sitting-room and breakfast-room. Bedrooms are passable, some brightly decorated, and vary in size; ask for one with a view across the rooftops and the steeple of Saint-Germain-des-Prés. We were of the opinion that the hotel has lost its bloom, and looks distinctly threadbare in places, although it still retains a long list of faithful customers.
Nearby blvd Saint-Germain; Musée d'Orsay; Louvre; Ile Saint-Louis; Latin Quarter.

■ 21 rue Jacob, 75006 Paris **Tel** (01) 43 25 30 60 **Fax** (01) 40 46 83 56
Location near junction with rue de Seine; **parking** rue Mazarine, blvd Saint-Germain; **metro** Saint-Germain-des-Prés, Mabillon **Meals** breakfast
Prices 580-1,100F; standard double 875F; breakfast 50F **Rooms** 37 double and twin and single, all with bath or shower; all rooms have phone, TV
Facilities conservatory, sitting-room, breakfast-room, lift, garden
Credit cards MV, V **Children** accepted **Disabled** no special facilities **Pets** not accepted **Closed** never **Proprietor** M. Henneveux

Saint-Germain-des-Prés

Le Relais Médicis

This gorgeous little hotel was opened in 1992 by the owners of the sought-after Relais Saint-Germain (see page 68), but inexplicably never became as successful as they had envisaged. In 1996 it was taken over by a husband-and-wife team, Monsieur and Madame Chérel, professional hoteliers who appear to have been successful in turning around its fortunes. Its 16 stylishly comfortable, beamed bedrooms, decorated in the style of different impressionist painters and all with luxurious marble bathrooms, are arranged around a pretty courtyard. On the ground floor everything is small-scale and dainty: a narrow entrance, a soothing little pink and green breakfast room and welcoming salon with dramatic red walls. Here they are covered with thoughtfully hung paintings. Prints or sepia photographs fill the walls elsewhere.
Nearby Latin Quarter; Musée de Cluny; Jardin de Luxembourg.

■ 23 rue Racine, 75006 Paris **Tel** (01) 43 26 00 60 **Fax** (01) 40 46 83 39
Location just off place de l'Odéon, between rue Corneille and rue Monsieur le Prince; **parking** rue l'Ecole de Médecine; metro Odéon; **Meals** breakfast
Prices 990-1,595F; standard double 1,395-1,495F; breakfast included
Rooms 16 double and twin, all with bath; all rooms have phone, TV, air conditioning, minibar, hairdrier **Facilities** sitting room, breakfast room, courtyard, lift **Credit cards** AE, DC, MC, V **Children** accepted **Disabled** not suitable **Pets** not accepted **Closed** never **Proprietors** M. and Mme Jean-Marie Chérel

Sixth Arrondissement

Saint-Germain-des-Prés

Hôtel de l'Odéon

Dominating each bedroom in this pleasant hotel is a different, but equally stunning, bed; it may be antique brass with inset pictures, a four-poster upholstered in tapestry, twin beds decorated with inlay and painted figures or a pretty wooden sleigh. There are antiques and mirrors to match. Housed in a beamed 16thC building, the *salon* is filled with antique and repro pieces; torch lights and paintings hang on the walls. Only the patterned carpet and tasteless fluorescent sign look out of place. There is a tiny, colourful garden and a breakfast-room, beyond which are the new bedrooms. Quieter, but smaller, these rooms have modern brass beds and pretty painted cupboards, but less character than the old. The reception staff are particularly friendly and welcoming.

Nearby blvd Saint-Germain; Jardin du Luxembourg; Ile de la Cité.

■ 13 rue Saint-Sulpice, 75006 Paris **Tel** (01) 43 25 70 11 **Fax** (01) 43 29 97 34 **Location** between rue de Condé and rue de Tournon; **parking** place Saint-Sulpice; **metro** Odéon, Mabillon **meals** breakfast **Prices** rooms 690-1,250F; standard double 850F; breakfast 60F **Rooms** 29; 21 double and twin, 4 single, 3 triple, 1 family, all with bath or shower; all rooms have phone, TV, air conditioning, hairdrier, safe **Facilities** sitting area, breakfast-room, lift **Credit cards** AE, DC, MC, V **Children** accepted **Disabled** possible, but no special facilities **Pets** accepted **Closed** never **Proprietor** M. Pilfert

Saint-Germain-des-Prés

Hôtel Prince de Conti

An upmarket, welcoming hotel which is perhaps too carefully designed, co-ordinated and generally coerced to generate much character, but nonetheless its bedrooms are very smart and comfortable. No. 61, for example, is a large room handsomely decked out in red and green Empire-style medallion wallpaper with chairs, carpet, curtains in matching colours. The ottoman at the end of the bed is a welcome extra touch. No. 42 is a pretty single, in pink *toile de jouy* with green furniture and a grey and black marble bathroom. The hotel has an identical twin close by, the **Prince de Condé** (39 rue de Seine; tel (01) 43 26 71 56), the only difference being that it boasts a luxury suite with Jacuzzi. Good breakfast.

Nearby blvd Saint-Germain; Sainte-Chapelle; Notre-Dame; Louvre.

■ 8 rue Guénégaud, 75006 Paris **Tel** (01) 44 07 30 40 **Fax** (01) 44 07 36 34 **Location** between rue Mazarine and quai de Conti; **parking** rue Mazarine; **metro** Odéon **Meals** breakfast **Prices** 910-1,400F; standard double 975F; breakfast 60-75F **Rooms** 26; 21 double and twin, 19 with bath, 2 with shower; 5 single, 4 with bath, one with shower; all rooms have phone, TV, air conditioning, minibar, hairdrier, safe **Facilities** sitting-room/breakfast-room, bar, courtyard, lift **Credit cards** AE, DC, MC, V **Children** accepted **Disabled** no special facilities but wide lift **Pets** accepted **Closed** never **Manager** Philippe Roye

Sixth Arrondissement

Saint-Germain-des-Prés

Hôtel Le Régent

For once a hotel where the bedrooms exceed the reception rooms. The lobby, with its mirrored walls, banks of houseplants and bright lighting lacks much character, but the recently renovated bedrooms are more interesting, all different, with unusually pretty bathrooms. Rooms at the back on the fifth and sixth floors have a view of Notre-Dame; larger ones have sitting areas. On the sixth floor, the large rooms at the front have their own tiny terraces. One has a lovely blue-and-white tiled bathroom; another has a damson pink tiled floor, with *toile de jouy* wallpaper in the bedroom.

Nearby blvd Saint-Germain; Latin Quarter; Sainte-Chapelle; Notre-Dame.

■ 61 rue Dauphine, 75006 Paris **Tel** (01) 46 34 59 80 **Fax** (01) 40 51 05 07 **Location** between rue Saint-André-des-Arts and rue Christine; **parking** rue Mazarine; **metro** Odéon **Meals** breakfast **Prices** 600-1,100F; standard double 750-1,100F; breakfast 60F **Rooms** 25; 20 double and twin, 16 with bath, 4 with shower; 5 single, all with shower; all rooms have phone, TV, air conditioning, minibar, trouser press (in large rooms), hairdrier, safe **Facilities** sitting area, breakfast-room, lift **Credit cards** AE, DC, MC, V **Children** accepted **Disabled** no special facilities **Pets** accepted **Closed** never **Manager** Mme Martin

Luxembourg Quarter

Régent's Hôtel

This used to be a plain, respectable two-star establishment with a low-key welcome, staid breakfast-room, and drab brown corridors. Since our last visit, however, a new proprietor has taken charge and has given the hotel a much-needed facelift, without greatly increasing the prices. Well located, close to the welcome open space of the Jardin du Luxembourg, there is also a flowery courtyard garden where you take breakfast on sunny mornings. We welcome hearing reports on the changes.

Nearby Jardin du Luxembourg; Saint-Sulpice; blvd Saint-Germain.

■ 44 rue Madame, 75006 Paris **Tel** (01) 45 48 02 81 **Fax** (01) 45 44 85 73 **Location** between rue Chevalier and rue de Vaugirard; **parking** Saint-Sulpice; **metro** Saint-Sulpice **Meals** breakfast **Prices** 400-800F; standard double 500F; breakfast 40F **Rooms** 37; 28 double, twin and triple, 4 family, 5 single, all with bath; all rooms have phone, TV, hairdrier **Facilities** breakfast-room, sitting area, courtyard garden, lift **Credit cards** AE, DC, MC, V **Children** accepted **Disabled** one room on ground floor **Pets** accepted **Closed** never **Proprietor** M Aymard

Sixth Arrondissement

Saint-Germain-des-Prés

Hôtel Saint-Germain-des-Prés

A small hotel with all the trappings, which stands out for charm and individuality, if not for notably good taste or coherence of interior design. Its bedrooms are all furnished in a hotchpotch of styles and colours; some have brightly coloured velvet bed-heads, others have vigorously floral wallpaper and fabric, which seems to overwhelm them; one suite has a solid four-poster, parquet floor, heavy wood furniture and tapestry-clad walls, and a Parisian scene in the bathroom. At the far end of the large *salon*-cum-breakfast-room a bank of fresh flowers introduces a riot of colour; unfortunately it fails to mask a chocolate-box mural in powdery pastels, depicting turn-of-the-century life in Saint-Germain. What you will find here is a friendly smile behind the reception desk and plenty of personal attention.
Nearby Musée d'Orsay; Louvre; blvd Saint-Germain; Ile de la Cité.

■ 36 rue Bonaparte, 75006 Paris **Tel** (01) 43 26 00 19 **Fax** (01) 40 46 83 63 **Location** between rue Jacob and rue de l'Abbaye; **parking** blvd Saint-Germain; **metro** Saint-Germain-des-Prés **Meals** breakfast **Prices** rooms 750-1,700F; standard double 980F; breakfast included **Rooms** 30; 28 double and twin, 2 suites, all with bath or shower; all rooms have phone, TV, minibar, hairdrier, safe; 15 rooms have air conditioning
Facilities sitting/breakfast-room, bar, lift **Credit cards** AE, MC, V
Children accepted **Disabled** no special facilities **Pets** accepted **Closed** never
Proprietor M. Nouvel

Saint-Germain-des-Prés

La Villa

Elegant rue Jacob is filled with richly stocked interior design and antique shops, which makes La Villa stand out all the more. Designed within an inch of its life to be ultra modern, ultra cool, its triple arched glass façade reveals a lobby with all the sophisticated minimalism, sensuous curves and hard edges that contemporary design requires. Upstairs, laser lights beam the room numbers on to the carpet in front of each door; behind them we find more unremitting modernity, softened by very soothing lights on dimmers, and glossy, high-tech bathrooms with stainless steel sinks set into frosted glass surrounds. Prices are high; service is polished.
Nearby blvd Saint-Germain; Musée d'Orsay; Louvre. Sainte-Chapelle; Notre-Dame.

■ 29 rue Jacob, 75006 Paris **Tel** (01) 43 26 60 00 **Fax** (01) 46 34 63 63 **Location** at junction with rue Bonaparte; **parking** blvd Saint-Germain (rue du Dragon); **metro** Saint-Germain-des-Prés **Meals** breakfast; room service **Prices** 850-3,000F; standard double 1,250-1,800F; breakfast 80F **Rooms** 32; 29 double and twin, 3 suites, all with bath; all rooms have phone, TV, air conditioning, minibar, hairdrier, safe **Facilities** breakfast-room, bar, lift, jazz bar **Credit cards** AE, DC, MC, V **Children** accepted **Disabled** access difficult **Pets** accepted **Closed** never **Manager** M. Leclercq

Sixth Arrondissement

Saint-Germain-des-Prés

Crystal Hôtel

Set in a little street filled with typical Left Bank restaurants, this is a family-run hotel which the owners strive to keep in good condition. The quiet rooms employ pretty fabrics and there is a large cellar breakfast-room with attractive glass-topped tables.

■ 24 rue Saint-Benoît, 75006 Paris **Tel** (01) 45 48 85 14 **Fax** (01) 45 49 16 45 **Meals** breakfast, brunch **Prices** 550-1,200F; standard double 712F; breakfast 40F **Rooms** 26; 17 double and twin, 4 single, 4 triple, one suite; 20 rooms with bath, 6 with shower; all rooms have phone, TV, minibar, hairdrier, safe **Credit cards** AE, DC, MC, V **Closed** never

Saint-Germain-des-Prés

Hôtel du Danube

Behind the wood-panelled and stone façade of this Napoleon III house, this friendly three-star is a touch too chintzy for our taste, but offers some better-than-adequate *chambres économiques*. They look on to an attractive courtyard and cost 650F a night – a bargain in rue Jacob. Pretty yellow and blue breakfast room.

■ 58 rue Jacob, 75006 Paris **Tel** (01) 42 60 34 70 **Fax** (01) 42 60 81 18 **Meals** breakfast **Prices** 650-1,150F; standard double 780-880F; breakfast 50F **Rooms** 40; 34 double and twin, 6 family, all with bath; all rooms have phone, TV, hairdrier **Credit cards** AE, MC, V **Closed** never

Saint-Germain-des-Prés

Hôtel Jardin de l'Odéon

There's nothing startling about this safe three-star hotel, except perhaps the geometric fabric on the *salon* sofas and chairs and the stiffish prices. The 1920s *leitmotif* extends from the green marble floor and smart black furniture to the posters and logo.

■ 7 rue Casimir-Delavigne, 75006 Paris **Tel** (01) 46 34 23 90 **Fax** (01) 43 25 28 12 **Meals** breakfast **Prices** rooms 440-1,218F; standard double 840-1,050F; breakfast 55F **Rooms** 41; 34 double and twin, 5 triple, all with bath; 2 single with shower; all rooms have phone, TV, minibar, hairdrier, safe **Credit cards** AE, MC, V **Closed** never

Luxembourg Quarter

Hôtel Perreyve

A pretty turn-of-the-century building across the street from the Régent's Hôtel (see page 120); both similar in simple sobriety and price, although Perreyve is cosier at breakfast in the homely *salon* – though bathrooms are less appealing, bedrooms smaller.

■ 63 rue Madame, 75006 Paris **Tel** (01) 45 48 35 01 **Fax** (01) 42 84 03 30 **Meals** breakfast; drinks **Prices** 440-620F; standard double 620F; breakfast 40F **Rooms** 30; 27 double and twin, 2 single, one triple, 13 with bath, 17 with shower; all rooms have phone, TV, hairdrier **Credit cards** AE, DC, MC, V **Closed** never

Sixth Arrondissement

Saint Germain-des Prés

Hôtel Saint-André-des-Arts

A one-off. If there are any beatniks left, this is the hotel for them. In the meantime, it endears itself to backpackers and academics who prefer the simple life. The house, in one of the liveliest streets in the district, dates from the late 16thC and has a charming old shop front as a façade, a splendid choirstall in the entrance and a listed staircase. After our latest visit, we felt that, despite a fresh lick of paint in the bedrooms, the common parts looked so shabby that we could no longer give the hotel a full entry. Prices are still unbeatable.

■ 66 rue Saint-André-des-Arts, 75006 Paris **Tel** (01) 43 26 96 16 **Fax** (1) 43 29 73 34 **Meals** breakfast **Prices** 380-660F; standard double 480F; breakfast included **Rooms** 33 single, double and twin, triple, family, all with bath or shower; all rooms have phone **Credit cards** MC, V **Closed** never

Saint-Germain-des-Prés/Latin Quarter

Relais-Hôtel du Vieux Paris

A building dating from 1480, this was a famous Beat Generation dive where the likes of Kerouac and Ginsberg searched for 'life and love in Paris' as one contemporary recently wrote in the visitors' book on a return visit. Now it is the obsession of Madame Odillard, who has lavished attention on the hotel, refurbishing all the prettily decorated, but over-priced, rooms.

■ 9 rue Gît-le-Coeur, 75006 Paris **Tel** (01) 43 54 41 66 **Fax** (01) 43 26 00 15 **Meals** breakfast **Prices** 1,090-1,800F; standard double 1,170F; breakfast 80F **Rooms** 13 double and twin, 9 with bath, 4 with shower, 7 suites; all rooms have phone, TV, air conditioning, minibar, hairdrier, safe **Credit cards** AE, DC, MC, V **Closed** never

Seventh Arrondissement

Saint-Germain-des-Prés

Hôtel de Beaune

It is easy to walk past this narrow 18thC house with its crumbling façade, and not notice that it's a hotel. But, once inside, the warm little interior envelopes you wholeheartedly. The dark red *moirée* walls and plain wood floor, bare but for one small runner, are part of a new decorative scheme created by the delightfully eccentric Madame Cholale. Beyond reception is a bar/breakfast area where banquettes are piled with cushions and guests can have coffee or breakfast at café tables. Bedrooms and bathrooms are adequate; some are surprisingly spacious and some share the idiosyncratic character of the ground floor.
Nearby Musée d'Orsay; Quai Voltaire; Louvre; blvd Saint-Germain.

■ 29 rue de Beaune, 75007 Paris **Tel** (01) 42 61 24 89 **Fax** (01) 49 27 02 12 **Location** between rue de l'Université and rue de Verneuil; **parking** rue Montalembert; **metro** rue du Bac, Solférino; **RER** Musée d'Orsay
Meals breakfast **Prices** rooms 419-750F; standard double 750F; breakfast 40F **Rooms** 19 double and twin, all with bath or shower; all rooms have phone, TV, minibar, hairdrier, safe **Facilities** bar/breakfast-room, lift **Credit cards** AE, DC, MC, V **Children** accepted **Disabled** not suitable **Pets** accepted **Closed** never **Proprietor** Mme Cholale

Saint-Germain-des-Prés

Hôtel Bersoly's Saint-Germain

A 17thC former convent, which has a great location for sightseeing. From the street, the entrance/*salon* looks cosy and inviting; a little beamed room with a stone floor and green walls, table lamps which cast a soft light, and sofa and chairs covered in a cheerful fabric. A pleasant place to wait, though its size causes problems if too many guests arrive at the same time. Sadly the warmth of the room did not extend to our welcome, which was distinctly cool. Each of the bedrooms – generally somewhat small too – has been thoughtfully tricked out in a favourite colour of the impressionist painter it is named after. Furniture is traditional; bathrooms, tiny and functional. Breakfast is served in a vaulted cellar, split into two separate rooms.
Nearby Musée d'Orsay; Quai Voltaire; Louvre; blvd Saint-Germain.

■ 28 rue de Lille, 75007 Paris **Tel** (01) 42 60 73 79 **Fax** (01) 49 27 05 55 **Location** between rue du Bac and rue des Saints-Pères; **parking** rue du Bac; **metro** rue du Bac, Saint-Germain-des-Prés; **RER** Musée d'Orsay
Meals breakfast **Prices** rooms 606-762F; standard double 762F; breakfast 50F **Rooms** 16 double and twin, all with bath or shower; all rooms have phone, TV, air conditioning, ceiling fan, hairdrier, safe **Facilities** sitting area, breakfast room, lift **Credit cards** MC, V **Children** accepted **Disabled** no special facilities **Pets** accepted **Closed** 2 weeks in Aug **Proprietor** Sylvie Carbonnaux

Seventh Arrondissement

Saint-Germain-des-Prés

Hôtel Montalembert

The decoration of this ritzy, costly hotel has been cleverly conceived and immaculately realized down to the last designer detail. Bannisters, lights and doorhandles, as well as principal pieces of furniture, have all been specially crafted in wrought iron, cast bronze, sycamore wood and leather. A bold navy and white striped fabric recurs on restaurant chair backs and duvets. The honey-marbled entrance looks stylish and important; the equally chic café/bar – definitely a place to be seen in – has a sitting area round an open fire at one end. Bedrooms are furnished with beautiful wooden beds and antiques or sleek black modern furniture – you can choose. Impeccable bathrooms have round chrome basins and shelves heaped with pristine monogrammed towels.

Nearby Musée d'Orsay; Louvre; blvd Saint-Germain.

■ 3 rue de Montalembert, 75007 Paris **Tel** (01) 45 49 68 68 **Fax** (01) 45 49 69 49 **Location** between rue de l'Université and blvd Saint-Germain, E off rue du Bac; **parking** underground car park next door; **metro** rue du Bac; **RER** Musée d'Orsay **meals** breakfast, lunch, dinner, room service **Prices** rooms 1,750-4,400F; standard double 2,300F; breakfast 100F; dinner from 225F **Rooms** 56; 51 double and twin, 5 suites, all with bath; all rooms have phone, fax/modem point, TV, video, air conditioning, minibar, hairdrier, safe **Facilities** bar/restaurant, sitting area, meeting rooms, lift **Credit cards** AE, DC, MC, V **Children** accepted **Disabled** no special facilities **Pets** accepted **Closed** never **Manager** M. Mercier

Invalides/Saint-Germain-des-Prés

Hôtel de Nevers

We recommend this quirky little hotel for the young and strong. It occupies a tall thin 17thC house, with no lift and stairs that seem to go up forever, and you're bound to have to carry your own bags. It has recently been redecorated and has an individual appeal, particularly in the tiny entrance with beams, one wall of rough stone and another mirrored to create the illusion of space. Close your eyes to the suspect artwork on the landings (where well-placed chairs invite you to sit and regain your breath) because if you can puff your way to the top, the bedrooms there have more than a little garret charm. Two on the first floor have huge windows. All afford terrific value for Saint-Germain.

Nearby blvd Saint-Germain; Musée d'Orsay; Musée Rodin.

■ 83 rue du Bac, 75007 Paris **Tel** (01) 45 44 61 30 **Fax** (01) 42 22 29 47 **Location** between rue de Grenelle and rue de Varenne; **parking** rue du Bac; **metro** rue du Bac, Sèvres Babylone; **RER** Musée d'Orsay **Meals** breakfast **Prices** rooms 430-530F; standard double 440-460F; breakfast 35F **Rooms** 11 double and twin, all with bath or shower, one single with shower; all rooms have phone, TV, minibar **Facilities** sitting area **Credit cards** not accepted **Children** accepted **Disabled** not suitable (no lift) **Pets** accepted **Closed** never **Proprietor** M. Hamrioui

Seventh Arrondissement

Saint-Germain-des-Prés

Hôtel du Quai Voltaire

A hotel since 1850, the Quai Voltaire has numbered Oscar Wilde, Wagner, Baudelaire and Pissaro amongst its guests. Its charm lies in its simplicity – it has changed little over the years – with spacious bedrooms mostly decorated with old-fashioned wallpapers and plain curtains. Each room is different and varies in size; those at the rear are quiet, while those at the front have a fabulous view across the Seine to the Louvre opposite. However, you pay a steep price for that view, both in terms of money (considering how basic the rooms are) and of noise – the windows are not soundproofed. A slow programme of redecoration is taking place to bring it up to date without, we hope, sacrificing its charm and sense of history.
Nearby Musée d'Orsay; Louvre; blvd Saint-Germain.

■ 19 Quai Voltaire, 75007 Paris **Tel** (01) 42 61 50 91 **Fax** (01) 42 61 62 26 **Location** bordering the Seine, mid-way between Pont-Royal and Pont du Carrousel; **parking** quai Anatole France; **metro** rue du Bac **Meals** breakfast, room service **Prices** 550-800F; standard double (with view) 700F; breakfast 45F **Rooms** 33; 25 double, 6 single, 2 triple; 27 rooms with bath, 4 with shower, 2 with washbasin (no WC); all rooms have phone, TV on request, hairdrier **Facilities** breakfast-room, sitting-room, lift **Credit cards** AE, DC, MC, V **Children** accepted **Disabled** access difficult **Pets** accepted **Closed** never **Proprietor** André Etchenique

Invalides/Eiffel Tower Quarter

Hôtel Thoumieux

In the shadow of the Eiffel Tower, this friendly place revolves around a bustling brasserie, which has belonged to the Thoumieux family since the 1930s, and is now run by Françoise and her husband, Jean Bassalert. Except for the addition of mirrored walls and modern prints, the cavernous restaurant, with its black fascia, dark red velvet curtains and banquettes, seems to have changed little since its opening. It specializes in country cuisine – *cassoulet, foie gras* and the like – and honest, drinkable house wines. The hotel entrance is to the right of the restaurant, and its stylish reception, on the first floor. Despite tasteful modern furniture, the spacious bedrooms remain slightly soulless. The large, airy breakfast-room can be hired for functions.
Nearby Invalides; Musée Rodin; blvd Saint-Germain; Eiffel Tower.

■ 79 rue Saint-Dominique, 75007 Paris **Tel** (01) 47 05 49 75 **Fax** (01) 47 05 36 96 **Location** between blvd Latour Maubourg and rue Amélie; **parking** Invalides; **metro** La Tour Maubourg, Invalides; **RER** Invalides, Pont de l'Alma **Meals** breakfast, lunch, dinner **Prices** 600-1,000F; standard double 600F; breakfast 45F; meals 82-200F **Rooms** 10 double and twin, all with bath; all rooms have phone, TV **Facilities** restaurant, breakfast-room **Credit cards** AE, MC **Children** accepted **Disabled** not suitable **Pets** accepted **Closed** never **Proprietors** Françoise Thoumieux and Jean Bassalert

Seventh Arrondissement

Invalides/Eiffel Tower Quarter

Hôtel Le Tourville

A plush four-star, under the same ownership as Le Saint-Grégoire (page 69), also designed by interior decorator Christian Badin. A brave combination of colours in the reception/*salon* – mint and dark green, royal blue, vivid orange – doesn't create harmony in this otherwise smart room. We liked the mix of antique and chic modern furniture, and the old books and sculptures dotted around. New carpets and redecoration has smartened up the corridors. Superior double rooms are particularly elegant, with white linen covers and black marble and grey tiled bathrooms. There are some lovely antiques in the bedrooms, but the odd table or bedside cabinet crops up looking as if it has come from a DIY store. A generous welcome from the anglophile manager.

Nearby Invalides; Musée Rodin; Musée de l'Armée; Eiffel Tower.

■ 16 ave de Tourville, 75007 Paris **Tel** (01) 47 05 62 62 **Fax** (01) 47 05 43 90 **Location** between blvd de La-Tour-Maubourg and ave de La Motte-Picquet; **parking** ave de Tourville; **metro** Ecole Militaire, La Tour Maubourg; **RER** Invalides **meals** breakfast **Prices** rooms 790-1,990F; standard double 890F; breakfast 60F **Rooms** 30; 28 double and twin, 2 suites, all with bath; all rooms have phone, TV, air conditioning, hairdrier **Facilities** bar, sitting-room, lift **Credit cards** AE, DC, MC, V **Children** accepted **Disabled** no special facilities **Pets** accepted **Closed** never **Proprietor** M. Bouvier

Invalides/Eiffel Tower Quarter

Hôtel de la Tulipe

Painted yellow and with its windows shaded by awnings, this hotel looks jolly from the outside, and doesn't disappoint within. Built in the mid 17thC for the wife of Louis XIV's gunpowder-keeper, after which it had a spell as a convent, it is now owned by a charming actor and his wife. The reception area is sunny and homely with sponged yellow walls, terracotta floor and pale beams. The much-needed breakfast-room, added recently, is equally attractive and bright. The upstairs bedrooms have recently been refurbished. The five rooms that lead off the pretty, overgrown courtyard are modest, but more private and appealing, at least in summer (in winter they may be a trifle damp).

Nearby Invalides; Musée Rodin; blvd Saint-Germain; Eiffel Tower.

■ 33 rue Malar, 75007 Paris **Tel** (01) 45 51 67 21 **Fax** (01) 47 53 96 37 **Location** between rue Saint-Dominique and rue de l'Université; **parking** Invalides; **metro** La Tour Maubourg, Invalides; **RER** Pont de l'Alma, Invalides **Meals** breakfast **Prices** rooms 550-650F; standard double 600F; breakfast 45F **Rooms** 22; 21 double and twin, all with bath or shower; one single with shower; all rooms have phone, TV, minibar **Facilities** sitting area, breakfast-room, courtyard garden **Credit cards** AE, MC, V **Children** accepted **Disabled** one specially adapted room available **Pets** accepted **Closed** never **Proprietors** M. and Mme Fortuit

Seventh Arrondissement

Saint-Germain-des-Prés

Hôtel de l'Académie

Smart hotel, rather stiffly decked out in a dark blue and green colour scheme with gilded Empire-style furniture and Classical statues adding a somewhat pompous note. The term 'junior suite' denotes a small sitting area and a Jacuzzi.

■ 32 rue des Saintes-Pères, 75007 Paris **Tel** (01) 45 48 36 22 **Fax** (01) 45 44 75 24 **Meals** breakfast **Prices** 490-1,590F; standard double 690-890F; breakfast 60F **Rooms** 33; 25 double and twin with bath, 8 single with shower; all rooms have phone, TV, minibar, hairdrier, safe; half have air conditioning **Credit cards** AE, DC, MC, V **Closed** never

Invalides /Eiffel Tower Quarter

Hôtel Relais Bosquet

Freshly decorated in shades of green and coral with cream walls, the Relais Bosquet unhappily lacks warmth, accentuated, on our visit, by one of the rudest receptionists we have encountered. It is and feels like part of a hotel chain. More reports please.

■ 19 rue du Champ de Mars, 75007 Paris **Tel** (01) 47 05 25 45 **Fax** (01) 45 55 08 24 **Meals** breakfast **Prices** rooms 550-700F; standard double 600F breakfast 30-57F **Rooms** 40 double and twin, all with bath; all rooms have phone, TV, minibar, tea/coffee making facilities, hairdrier, safe **Credit cards** AE, DC, MC, V **Closed** never

Invalides /Eiffel Tower Quarter

Hôtel du Cadran

The glass and brass revolving door gives the impression of a business hotel, but the du Cadran has more appeal than that. Modern furnishings blend with occasional antiques and a 17thC working fireplace. Bedrooms are comfy, but uniform and smallish.

■ 10 rue du Champ de Mars, 75007 Paris **Tel** (01) 40 62 67 00 **Fax** (01) 40 62 67 13 **Meals** breakfast **Prices** rooms 850-1,620F; standard double 850F; breakfast 55F **Rooms** 42 double and twin, all with bath; all rooms have phone, TV, air conditioning, minibar, safe **Credit cards** AE, DC, MC, V **Closed** never

Saint-Germain-des-Prés

Hôtel de Lille

The reception area is sparse, but quite smart, with a marble floor, blue tub chairs and black-and-white pictures. Bedrooms, bathrooms and corridors have been repainted. Spiral stairs lead down to a distinctly 1970s vaulted breakfast/sitting-room.

■ 40 rue de Lille, 75007 Paris **Tel** (01) 42 61 29 09 **Fax** (01) 42 61 53 97 **Meals** breakfast **Prices** rooms 520-880F; standard double 610F; breakfast included **Rooms** 20; 13 double and twin, all with bath or shower; 6 single with shower; one triple with bath; all rooms have phone, TV, hairdrier, safe **Credit cards** AE, DC, MC, V **Closed** never

Seventh Arrondissement

Invalides Quarter

Hôtel de Suède

A popular, traditional, good-value hotel in the embassy district. Pleasant bedrooms, recently renovated, and with new bathrooms, have high beds and velvet chairs; some overlook the gardens of the Prime Minister's official residence. Downstairs the decoration is of more dubious taste. Walls are panelled in an orange-ish wood veneer, which clashes with the grey carpet and gold velvet chairs. It has a small courtyard garden.

■ 31 rue Vaneau, 75007 Paris **Tel** (01) 47 05 00 08 **Fax** (01) 47 05 69 27 **Meals** breakfast, room service **Prices** rooms 506-1,200F; standard double 752F; breakfast 50F **Rooms** 39; 35 double and twin, all with bath or shower; 4 single with shower; all rooms have phone; 35 rooms have TV **Credit cards** AE, MC, V **Closed** never

Invalides Quarter

Hôtel de Varenne

You stumble upon this little hotel through its agreeably overgrown 'secret' garden. The pleasing entrance has cream walls, white-painted panelling and a corniced ceiling, a tiled floor and well-placed mirrors and plants. Since our last visit, the breakfast-room and bedrooms have been spruced up. Bathrooms are mostly spacious, and the staff are friendly and helpful.

■ 44 rue de Bourgogne, 75007 Paris **Tel** (01) 45 51 45 55 **Fax** (01) 45 51 86 63 **Meals** breakfast **Prices** rooms 610-740F; standard double 710F; breakfast 50F **Rooms** 24; 20 double and twin, all with bath; 4 single with shower; all rooms have phone, TV, hairdrier, safe **Credit cards** AE, MC, V **Closed** never

Eighth Arrondissement

Champs-Elysées

Hôtel Centre Ville Matignon

A perfect recreation of the Art Deco period from the sweep of the reception desk and the mosaic-tiled floor in the little entrance to the large square basins in the bathrooms where every square inch is tiled. There is a pretty gilded fountain on the left as you come in, but the *pièce de résistance* is the lift, a narrow cage with a decorated opaque glass exterior door. It looks stunning and is the genuine article, but hardly practical when a family of four arrives with all their luggage. The bedrooms tend to be small and slightly shabby with dark, if carefully chosen, fabrics. The hotel has an arrangement with the bar next door, which is under different management, allowing guests to have breakfast there.
Nearby Champs-Elysées; Grand Palais; Petit Palais; ave Montaigne.

■ 3 rue de Ponthieu, 75008 Paris **Tel** (01) 42 25 73 01 **Fax** (01) 42 56 01 39 **Location** between ave Matignon and rue Jean Mermoz; **parking** ave Matignon, Rond-Point des Champs-Elysées; **metro** Franklin D. Roosevelt; **RER** Charles de Gaulle Etoile **Meals** breakfast **Prices** 590-1,200F; standard double 690-890F; breakfast 55F **Rooms** 23; 19 double and twin, all with bath or shower; 4 junior suites with bath; all rooms have phone, TV, air conditioning, minibar, hairdrier, safe **Facilities** sitting area, lift **Credit cards** AE, DC, MC, V **Children** accepted **Disabled** access difficult **Pets** accepted **Closed** never **Proprietor** M. Michaud

Champs-Elysées

Hôtel Franklin Roosevelt

Murals are the special feature of the Franklin Roosevelt: when you book, ask for one of the bedrooms with a Zuber-inspired South Seas colonial scene. They lend a delightful sense of calm. Bedrooms differ in style; some have a Japanese theme; others are decorated in pastels, with chintz, checked or elegant cream curtains; most are spacious, with large bathrooms. Three suites and eight 'de-luxe' rooms have been created since our last visit.

Downstairs, there are more murals in the delicate *salon* and in the little breakfast-room, where the flower-entwined trellises echo the terrace outside with its *trompe l'oeil* garden and stunning camellias in tubs. Only the masculine English-style bar has escaped the mural treatment.
Nearby Champs-Elysées; Grand Palais; Petit Palais; ave Montaigne.

■ 18 rue Clément-Marot, 75008 Paris **Tel** (01) 53 57 49 50 **Fax** (01) 47 20 44 30 **Location** between rue Marbeuf and rue de La Trémoille; **parking** rue François 1er, rue Marbeuf, ave George V; **metro** Franklin D. Roosevelt, Alma-Marceau, George V **Meals** breakfast **Prices** rooms 895-3,000F; standard double 945F; breakfast 65F **Rooms** 45 double and twin, all with bath or shower; all rooms have phone, TV, minibar, hairdrier, safe **Facilities** sitting-room, bar, breakfast-room, patio garden, lift **Credit cards** AE, MC, V **Children** accepted **Disabled** access difficult **Pets** accepted **Closed** never **Proprietor** M. Leboudec

Eighth Arrondissement

Champs-Elysées

Hôtel Résidence Lord Byron

In an area of grand hotels and exorbitant prices, the Lord Byron – slightly more illustrious sister of the Mayflower next door (see below) – stands out for its personal service and, by local standards, reasonable prices. The elegant entrance and formal sitting-room are decorated to a high standard in traditional style, with a fleet of delicate chairs, upholstered in velvet or checked silk. With the exception of the suites, bedrooms tend to be smallish, but are modern and comfortable, with bold floral fabrics, a mix of old and new furnishings and spotless bathrooms. Misconceived wall-coverings range from grasspaper to anaglypta. Annexe bedrooms – across a flower-filled garden – offer peace and quiet.
Nearby Arc de Triomphe; Champs-Elysées; Musée Jacquemart-André.

■ 5 rue Chateaubriand, 75008 Paris **Tel** (01) 43 59 89 98 **Fax** (01) 42 89 46 04 **Location** between rue Washington and rue Lord Byron; **parking** ave de Friedland, Champs-Elysées, rue de Berri; **metro** George V, Charles de Gaulle Etoile; **RER** Charles de Gaulle Etoile **meals** breakfast **Prices** rooms 700-1,300F; standard double 820-920F; breakfast 55F **Rooms** 31; 23 double and twin, 6 suites, all with bath or shower; 2 single with shower; all rooms have phone, TV, minibar, hairdrier, safe **Facilities** sitting/meeting room, breakfast-room, garden, lift **Credit cards** AE, DC, MC, V **Children** accepted **Disabled** no special facilities **Pets** not accepted **Closed** never **Proprietor** Mme Benoit

Champs-Elysées

Hôtel Mayflower

A friendly hotel in the same ownership as the Résidence Lord Byron next door (see above), with a similarly refined and relaxed atmosphere. The bar/*salon* is a restful place to put up your feet at the end of a tiring day. Bedrooms are pretty, with chintz fabric and limed or stained wood furniture, but some on the street are noisy and cramped. Those on the courtyard side have large bathrooms and are pricier, but still value for money, considering the location. The cellar breakfast-room is a refreshing variation on the theme: it is done out like an ocean liner with a seascape mural on one wall, and not a rough-stone wall or copper pot in sight. Ugly grasspaper in the corridors is in need of renovation.
Nearby Arc de Triomphe; Champs-Elysées; Musée Jacquemart-André.

■ 3 rue Chateaubriand, 75008 Paris **Tel** (01) 45 62 57 46 **Fax** (01) 42 56 32 38 **Location** between rue Washington and rue Lord Byron; **parking** ave de Friedland, Champs-Elysées, rue de Berri; **metro** George V, Charles de Gaulle Etoile; **RER** Charles de Gaulle Etoile **Meals** breakfast **Prices** rooms 660-970F; standard double 820-970F; breakfast 50F **Rooms** 24; 18 double and twin, all with bath; 6 single with bath or shower; all rooms have phone, TV, minibar, hairdrier, safe **Facilities** bar/sitting-room, breakfast-room, lift **Credit cards** AE, MC, V **Children** accepted **Disabled** no special facilities **Pets** accepted **Closed** never **Proprietor** Mme Benoit

Eighth Arrondissement

Opéra

Hôtel Queen Mary

The tell-tale signs that this hotel is British owned, apart from the name and the carriage lamps that flank the front door, are the trouser press in every room and the full English breakfast available each morning. Following a rigorous and total renovation, this well-appointed three-star, decorated throughout in cream, pale yellow and peach, or yellow combined with blue, is kept well up to scratch. But, despite this and some attractive original cornicing, it lacks panache. Bedrooms – single, standard and superior double – are fresh and comfortable, but uniform, with reproduction furniture. In summer, you can sit out on the pretty terrace.
Nearby Madeleine; Opéra Garnier; place Vendôme; Jardin des Tuileries.

■ 9 rue de Greffulhe, 75008 Paris **Tel** (01) 42 66 40 50 **Fax** (01) 42 66 94 92 **Location** between rue des Mathurins and rue de Castellane; **parking** place de la Madeleine, blvd Haussmann, blvd Malesherbes; **metro** Havre Caumartin, Madeleine, Saint-Augustin; **RER** Auber **Meals** breakfast, room service **Prices** rooms 755-1,300F; standard double 875F; breakfast 75F **Rooms** 36; 30 double and twin, one suite, all with bath; 5 single with shower; all rooms have phone, TV, air conditioning, minibar, trouser press, hairdrier, safe **Facilities** sitting-room, bar, breakfast-room, patio garden, lift **Credit cards** AE, MC, V **Children** accepted **Disabled** access possible **Pets** accepted **Closed** never **Proprietor** David Byrne

Champs-Elysées

Hôtel San Regis

Just a stiletto's step from avenue Montaigne, home to Christian Dior, Valentino and other great names of fashion, the elegantly opulent San Regis has been patronized by couturiers since it opened in 1923. On the ground floor is a smart little restaurant, lined with *faux* books, and an adjacent glossy bar. Bedrooms have richly coloured, though sometimes over-patterned, fabrics, deep sofas, antiques and impeccable bathrooms – every one equipped with a phone, so you can order a glass of champagne as you soak. Staff are wonderfully attentive, but you are paying for it.
Nearby Champs-Elysées; ave Montaigne; Grand Palais; Petit Palais; Place de la Concorde; the Seine.

■ 12 rue Jean-Goujon, 75008 Paris **Tel** (01) 44 95 16 16 **Fax** 45 61 05 48 **Location** between ave Franklin D. Roosevelt and place François 1er; **parking** imp. d'Antin; **metro** Franklin D. Roosevelt, Champs-Elysées Clemenceau **meals** breakfast, lunch, dinner, room service **Prices** 1,650-5,500F; standard double 2,200F; breakfast 110F; dinner from 250F **Rooms** 44; 42 double, twin and suites, all with bath; 2 single with shower; all rooms have phone, TV, air conditioning, minibar, hairdrier **Facilities** sitting area, sitting-room, restaurant, bar, lift **Credit cards** AE, DC, MC, V **Children** accepted **Disabled** not suitable **Pets** not accepted **Closed** never **Manager** M. George

Eighth Arrondissement

Champs-Elysées

Hôtel Bradford

The renovation that was taking place at the time of our last visit is now complete and we hope it hasn't spoiled the old-fashioned charm of this hotel. Many double rooms are vast, with 50s-style furniture. Armoires full of linen stand in creaky corridors. Original features such as the flag-stone floor in the hall and the ornately carved wooden lift have been preserved. Breakfast can now be taken in the new conservatory.

■ 10 rue Saint-Philippe du Roule, 75008 Paris **Tel** (01) 45 63 20 20 **Fax** (01) 45 63 20 07 **Meals** breakfast, room service **Prices** rooms 990-1,690F; standard double 1,290F; breakfast 90F **Rooms** 51; 42 double and twin, 7 single, one family, all with bath or shower; all rooms have phone, TV, minibar, hairdrier, safe **Credit cards** AE, DC, MC, V **Closed** never

Champs-Elysées

Hôtel Claridge-Bellman

A miniature Claridges, which boasts a loyal *clientèle* (mostly business people), attracted by the manager's warm welcome, the handsome bar/restaurant and traditional style, established with velvet Second Empire chairs, tapestries, oil paintings and chandeliers. Bedrooms in browns and apricots with dark furniture have a masculine feel; some of the dated bathrooms have been renewed.

■ 37 rue François 1er, 75008 Paris **Tel** (01) 47 23 54 42/47 23 90 03 **Fax** (01) 47 23 08 84 **Meals** breakfast, lunch, dinner **Prices** rooms 900-1,600F; standard double 1,400F; breakfast 85F; dinner from 225F **Rooms** 42; 35 double and twin, all with bath or shower; 7 single with bath; all rooms have phone, TV, air conditioning, minibar, trouser press, hairdrier **Credit cards** AE, DC, MC, V **Closed** never

Ninth Arrondissement

Opéra Quarter

Hôtel de Beauharnais

Tucked away down a long, rather dull street, this is a quaint budget establishment, dominated by its splendid owner, Madame Bey. On our visit, she proudly flung back the sheets to reveal pristine mattresses, and insisted on lifting the loo seats and the pedal bin lids. "I am German," she announced, "and I like everything to be completely clean." Rooms are furnished with an eclectic mix of Victorian antiques, some delightfully over-the-top – for instance a massive wooden bedstead, a collection of Venetian glass wall lights, and a large number of ornate and over-sized mirrors. Downstairs, there is a new reception area. The excellent breakfast coffee is another source of pride: "It is *very good*," she states, "because I make it *as at home*, you understand?"

Nearby Opéra Garnier; Grands Boulevards; Gare Saint-Lazare; La Madeleine.

■ 51 rue de la Victoire, 75009 Paris **Tel** (01) 48 74 71 13 **Fax** (01) 44 53 98 80 **Location** N of rue La Fayette, between rue de la Chaussée and rue Lafitte; **parking** in street; **metro** Chaussée d'Antin **Meals** breakfast **Prices** 405-580F; standard double 400-480F; breakfast 30F **Rooms** 17; 11 double and twin, 5 single, 1 family, all with shower, 13 with WC; most rooms have hairdrier **Facilities** breakfast room, lift **Credit cards** not accepted **Children** accepted **Disabled** access difficult **Pets** accepted **Closed** never **Proprietors** Mme and Mlle Bey

Opéra Quarter

Hôtel du Léman

Ivy climbs the trellis-work between the windows and flower-filled baskets hang from the balconies on the pretty exterior of this hotel. Inside, the marble-floored entrance is uncluttered with diverse objects including an Egyptian sculpture and a slim uplighter, both strategically placed. The bedrooms are decorated in muted shades, with stained wood bedheads and small functional bathrooms, and though tasteful, are impersonal. The most congenial rooms are those on the sixth floor, where sloping walls and beams give them some character. The cellar breakfast-room has rough-stone walls and looks like a hundred others in the city, only more kitsch, with café tables and chairs, and some garish paintings.

Nearby Folies Bergères; Gare du Nord; Opéra Garnier; Montmartre; Musée Grévin.

■ 20 rue de Trévise, 75009 Paris **Tel** (01) 42 46 50 66 **Fax** (01) 48 24 27 59 **Location** between rue Richer and rue Sainte-Cécile; **parking** in street or rue Richer, rue Bleue; **metro** rue Montmartre, Cadet, Bonne Nouvelle **Meals** breakfast, brunch **Prices** rooms 410-540F; standard double 540-660F; breakfast, brunch 45F **Rooms** 24 double and twin, all with bath; all rooms have phone, TV, minibar, hairdrier, safe **Facilities** sitting area, breakfast-room, lift **Credit cards** AE, DC, MC, V **Children** accepted **Disabled** access difficult **Pets** accepted **Closed** never **Proprietor** Emmanuelle Le Grand

Ninth Arrondissement

Opéra/Montmartre

Hôtel Riboutté-Lafayette

There is nothing pretentious about this modest, inexpensive two-star, around the corner from the Folies-Bergères and more like a hotel in the provinces than one in the centre of Paris. In the homely reception area there is space to sit at tables on rush-seated chairs, or to relax in deep cane sofas. The glow from several pretty table lamps accentuates the warm ambience, and care has been taken with flower arrangements and little pieces of china on display. Presiding over it all is the delightful Claudine Gourd, manager here since 1972, and her faithful 13-year-old scottie, Chipie. Bedrooms tend to be small and unexceptional, though ones at the top have beams, and some have pleasing pieces of painted furniture.
Nearby Gare du Nord; Opéra Garnier; Grands Boulevards.

■ 5 rue de Ribouttè, 75009 Paris **Tel** (01) 47 70 62 36 **Fax** (01) 48 00 91 50 **Location** S of square de Montholon, between rue La Fayette and rue Bleue; **parking** in street or square de Montholon, Cité de Trévise, rue Richer; **metro** Cadet, Poissonnière; **RER** Gare du Nord **Meals** breakfast, room service **Prices** rooms 300-465F; standard double 400-460F; breakfast 25-35F **Rooms** 24; 18 double and twin, 5 triple, all with bath or shower; one single with shower; all rooms have phone, TV, hairdrier **Facilities** sitting/breakfast area, lift **Credit cards** AE, MC, V **Children** accepted **Disabled** not suitable **Pets** accepted **Closed** never **Proprietor** M. Pannard

Opéra/Montmartre

Hôtel de La Tour d'Auvergne

Neither the tame façade on a pretty cobbled street, nor the smart hall with its marble floor and coral chairs, prepares you for what lies in store upstairs. Each bedroom was conceived and decorated by Eliane Duval, mother of the present owner, and ranges from the chic – navy and white, or pale blue checks – to the outrageous – a mix of lime green designs with matching carpet, or a room done up entirely in pinky *toile de jouy*; not just curtains, but bedspread, bedhead, canopy, walls and ceiling too. Beds are almost all canopied and, though over the top, the look is unfaltering and prices are very reasonable. Bathrooms are white-tiled with a refreshing hint of colour. The basement breakfast-room has bold silvery walls, in which shimmers a reflective blur of white café tables and chairs.
Nearby Gare du Nord; Opéra Garnier; Grands Boulevards.

■ 10 rue de la Tour-d'Auvergne, 75009 Paris **Tel** (01) 48 78 61 60 **Fax** (01) 49 95 99 00 **Location** between rue de Rochechouart and rue Rodier; **parking** in street or square d'Anvers; **metro** Anvers, Cadet; **RER** Gare du Nord **Meals** breakfast **Prices** 500-750F; standard double 550-700F; breakfast 55F **Rooms** 25; 18 double and twin, 4 single, 3 triple, all with bath or shower; all rooms have phone, TV, hairdrier, safe **Facilities** sitting area/bar, breakfast-room, lift **Credit cards** AE, DC, MC, V **Children** accepted **Disabled** not suitable **Pets** accepted **Closed** never **Proprietor** M. Duval

Twelfth Arrondissement

Nation

Nouvel Hôtel

If you're on a budget and don't mind being some way from the centre, you could do worse than this simple, friendly two-star. Staying here feels more like being a guest in a private house than a hotel. One of its greatest assets is a sweet garden, crowded with trees and flowers. Inside, the decoration has an old-fashioned charm: the breakfast-room is encircled by a painted garland of fruit, tables are swathed in floral cloths, and antique metal lights hang from corridor ceilings. Fresh and flowery, the bedrooms are all different, with handsome painted furniture and small, functional bathrooms through sliding doors. Communicating rooms can accommodate families of up to four. **Nearby** Gare de Lyon; place de la Bastille; Opéra de Paris Bastille (all a brisk walk away).

■ 24 ave du Bel Air, 75012 Paris **Tel** (01) 43 43 01 81 **Fax** (01) 43 44 64 13 **Location** between place de la Nation and rue du Pensionnat; **parking** ave de Saint-Mandé; **metro** Nation, Picpus; **RER** Nation **meals** breakfast **Prices** rooms 360-550F; standard double 380-415F; breakfast 40F **Rooms** 28; 25 double and twin, 3 triple, all with bath or shower; all rooms have phone, TV **Facilities** sitting/breakfast-room, garden **Credit cards** AE, DC, MC, V **Children** accepted **Disabled** access difficult **Pets** accepted **Closed** never **Proprietors** Claude and Danielle Marillier

Bois de Vincennes

Hôtel de la Porte Dorée

A pre-war time warp, in the same ownership for the past 60 years. Original wooden staircase, splendid panelled walls, ancient radiators. Smaller bedrooms are spacious, larger ones are huge, plain and light, augmented by neat little bathrooms. The breakfast-room owes more to a quiet suburban home than to a hotel.

■ 273 Ave Daumesnil, 75012 Paris **Tel** (01) 43 07 56 97 **Fax** (01) 49 28 08 18 **Meals** breakfast **Prices** rooms 275-300F; standard double 300F; breakfast 28F **Rooms** 40 double and twin, 5 with bath, 35 with shower; all rooms have phone, TV, hairdrier **Credit cards** AE, MC, V **Closed** never

Fourteenth Arrondissement

Montparnasse

Hôtel Raspail Montparnasse

A hotel on the busy boulevard Raspail that harks back to the 1920s – the cultural heyday of Montparnasse. Beneath the original *marquise* and garland of carved roses, the entrance is through heavy glass doors with chrome Art Deco handles, which swing open automatically to let you in to an airy reception/sitting-room. Here scarlet leather and grey velvet tub chairs cluster around small tables, on which rest spindly black lamps. The design is the work of celebrated decorator Serge Pons. Fabulous photographs line the walls, and art and sculpture is sometimes exhibited. Bedrooms in different colours pay homage to individual artists: Cézanne, Chagall, Modigliani and Picasso, among others. Chic, but hard-edged, it appeals to business types.
Nearby Jardin du Luxembourg; Cimetière du Montparnasse.

■ 203 blvd Raspail, 75014 Paris **Tel** (01) 43 20 62 86 **Fax** (01) 43 20 50 79
Location at southern junction of blvd Montparnasse and blvd Raspail; **parking** blvd du Montparnasse; **metro** Vavin; **RER** Port Royal
Meals breakfast **Prices** rooms 520-1,160F; standard double 730-890F; breakfast 50F **Rooms** 38; 33 double and twin, 5 single, all with bath or shower; all rooms have phone, TV, air conditioning, minibar, hairdrier, safe
Facilities bar/sitting area, meeting room, lift **Credit cards** AE, MC, V
Children accepted **Disabled** no special facilities **Pets** not accepted
Closed never **Proprietor** Christiane Martinent

Montparnasse

Hôtel de Blois

One large table, covered in a floral cloth, stands in the breakfast-cum-sitting-room, making this simple hotel feel more like a home. The bedrooms are just as modest as the ground floor rooms, though some have lovely big old beds.

■ 5 rue des Plantes, 75014 Paris **Tel** (01) 45 40 99 48 **Fax** (01) 45 40 45 62 **Meals** breakfast **Prices** rooms 230-360F; standard double 360F; breakfast 25F **Rooms** 26 double, twin and triple; 15 with bath or shower; 9 with WC; all rooms have phone; some rooms have TV **Credit cards** AE, MC, V **Closed** never

Montparnasse

Hôtel Lenox Montparnasse

The sister hotel of the Lenox Saint-Germain (see page 74) pales into insignificance compared to its far more alluring sibling. Atmosphere is lacking in both the sophisticated but dull bedrooms and the public rooms; best is the handsome bar where light meals are also served.

■ 15 rue Delambre, 75014 Paris **Tel** (01) 43 35 34 50 **Fax** (01) 43 20 46 64
Meals breakfast, room service **Prices** 640-1,500F; standard double 640F; breakfast 45F **Rooms** 52, included double and twin, single and mini suite, 44 with bath, 8 with shower; all rooms have phone, TV, hairdrier
Credit cards AE, DC, MC, V **Closed** never

Fifteenth Arrondissement

Eiffel Tower Quarter

L'Hôtel du Bailli de Suffren

Small but significant details lift this hotel, named after a famous admiral, above the three-star norm. The *salon* is filled with well-chosen antiques, and pictures and sculptures that are for sale. The owner clearly wants to please: an open book invites comments and there are questionnaires in the bedrooms. Robes are provided, as well as cotton wool and nail files. Bedrooms and bathrooms all have different colour schemes (we preferred the pale to the dark), and bedside lights are on dimmers. Double rooms can combine to form apartments. Breakfast is served in a pleasant pink and green room. Drawbacks are that the area is rather unappealing, and, while we were there, the huge television blared constantly in the *salon*.

Nearby Eiffel Tower; UNESCO; Ecole Militaire; Invalides.

■ 149 ave de Suffren, 75015 Paris **Tel** (01) 56 58 64 64 **Fax** (01) 45 67 75 82 **Location** between rue Pérignon and rue Bellart; **parking** rue François Bonvin; **metro** Ségur, Sèvres Lecourbe, Cambronne **Meals** breakfast, light meals **Prices** rooms 685-1,500F; standard double 780F; continental breakfast 45F, buffet breakfast 65F **Rooms** 25; 15 double and twin, 5 triple, all with bath; 5 single with shower; all rooms have phone, TV, hairdrier, safe **Facilities** sitting-room, breakfast-room, lift **Credit cards** AE, DC, MC, V **Children** accepted **Disabled** no special facilities **Pets** accepted **Closed** never **Proprietor** M. Tardif

Eiffel Tower Quarter

Hôtel Charles Quinze

An acceptable two-star, if you don't mind the dull area, some way from the city centre. The entrance is quite agreeable, filled with pine furniture and dark blue leather chairs which counter the sterile effect of a white-tiled floor. Bedrooms have been redecorated recently and have modern bathrooms and contemporary pictures. There's a basement breakfast room, and a terrace garden for use in summer.

■ 37 rue Saint-Charles-36 rue Rouelle, 75015 Paris **Tel** (01) 45 79 64 15 **Fax** (01) 45 77 21 11 **Meals** breakfast **Prices** rooms 425-590F; standard double 520F; breakfast 45F **Rooms** 30; 25 double and twin, all with bath or shower; 5 single with shower; all rooms have phone, TV, minibar, hairdrier **Credit cards** AE, DC, MC, V **Closed** never

Sixteenth Arrondissement

Chaillot Quarter

Hôtel du Bois

Up a short flight of stairs in the little cobbled rue du Dôme, the exterior is alluring – white stucco with black wrought-iron balconies and railings, hung with geranium-filled window boxes. This popular hotel, a step from the Arc de Triomphe, is in the same English ownership as the Queen Mary (see page 132). The winter of 1996 saw the total refurbishment of bedrooms and public rooms, and the du Bois' upgrading to three stars. The slightly fusty brown paisley print and leather furniture have been jettisoned in favour of pale yellow walls with dashes of bright red in the furnishings, reproduction antiques and a marble floor, strewn – here and there – with rugs. Bedrooms are comfortable, though nothing special, with double glazing, gleaming bathrooms, and co-ordinated fabrics. The feel is very similar to that of its sister hotel.
Nearby Arc de Triomphe; Champs-Elysées; Trocadéro; Musé National d'Ennery; Musée Armenian.

■ 11 rue du Dôme, 75116 Paris **Tel** (01) 45 00 31 96 **Fax** (01) 45 00 90 05 **Location** between ave Victor Hugo and rue Lauriston; **parking** rue Lauriston, ave Victor Hugo; **metro** Charles de Gaulle Etoile, Kléber, Victor Hugo; **RER** Charles de Gaulle Etoile **Meals** breakfast **Prices** rooms 525-685F; standard double 595F; breakfast 55F **Rooms** 41; 37 double and twin, all with bath or shower; 4 single with shower; all rooms have phone, TV, minibar, safe **Facilities** breakfast/sitting-room **Credit cards** AE, MC, V **Children** accepted **Disabled** no special facilities **Pets** not accepted **Closed** never **Proprietor** David Byrne

Chaillot Quarter

Hôtel Majestic

Don't judge this hotel by its ugly, modern façade, because the interior justifies its name. In reception, a fine black and white marble floor is strewn with rugs. Upstairs, heavy doors open off landings on to vast, comfortable bedrooms, many with dark red carpets, old-fashioned chintzes, king-size beds and pre-war furniture. Bathrooms are also large; some, old; others, brand new and strangely out of place, though even these have big old style basins. The public rooms are equally formal, with velvet chairs, potted plants and *trompe l'oeil* doors. A slightly faded old lady of a hotel, where you can imagine eating cucumber sandwiches and sipping tea with a great aunt. The penthouse apartment looks even more dated, but is huge, with its own terrace.
Nearby Arc de Triomphe; Champs-Elysées; Trocadéro; Musée de la Mode et du Costume Palais Galliera.

■ 29 rue Dumont d'Urville, 75116 Paris **Tel** (01) 45 00 83 70 **Fax** (01) 45 00 29 48 **Location** between rue Jean Giraudoux and rue de Belloy; **parking** in street or ave Foch, Champs-Elysées; **metro** Kléber, Boissière Charles de Gaulle Etoile; **RER** Charles de Gaulle Etoile **Meals** breakfast **Prices** rooms 1,050-2,200F; standard double 1,350F; breakfast 70F **Rooms** 30; 27 double and twin, 2 suites, one penthouse apartment, all with bath; all rooms have phone, TV, air conditioning, minibar **Facilities** sitting areas, sitting-room, lift **Credit cards** AE, DC, MC, V **Children** accepted **Disabled** no special facilities **Pets** accepted **Closed** never **Manager** Mme Baverez

Sixteenth Arrondissement

Passy

Hôtel Massenet

In the residential district of Passy, the Massenet cuts an eccentric figure with its green marble floor, wood-panelled walls, hunting prints, leather sofas and chairs, and *Herald Tribune* in the rack. The bedrooms cast off this masculine air; typically they are decorated in subtle colours with cream and gold furniture and brocade curtains and bedspreads. There's a private celadon-coloured sitting-room, and a bar that's open round the clock. Guests eat breakfast in a grey room with flower prints, leather chairs and original cornicing, or on the charming sliver of a terrace when the weather is clement.

■ 5 bis rue Massenet, 75016 Paris **Tel** (01) 45 24 43 03 **Fax** (01) 45 24 41 39 **Meals** breakfast **Prices** rooms 520-790F; standard double 790F; breakfast 45F **Rooms** 41; 31 double and twin, 10 single, all with bath or shower; all rooms have phone, TV, minibar, hairdrier; some have air conditioning **Credit cards** AE, DC, MC, V **Closed** never

Passy

Le Hameau de Passy

This hotel's best feature is its situation in a secluded little courtyard, planted with trees and flowers, and set back from rue de Passy and its traffic noise. The old shuttered façade would be attractive but for the glass-encased spiral staircases which have been tacked on to it. These lead to modern bedrooms (a lift serves some too), all faintly soulless with white rough-cast walls and painted wooden furniture. On the ground floor there's a place to sit within the reception area and a breakfast room.

■ 48 rue de Passy, 75016 Paris **Tel** (01) 42 88 47 55 **Fax** (01) 42 30 83 72 **Meals** breakfast, light meals **Prices** rooms 550-705F; standard double 600-620F; breakfast included; 10F if served in rooms **Rooms** 32; 29 double and twin (3 can be triple), 19 with bath, 10 with shower; 4 single, 3 with bath, one with shower; all rooms have phone, TV, air conditioning **Credit cards** AE, DC, MC, V **Closed** never

Porte Maillot

La Villa Maillot

Occupying the former Sierre Leone Embassy, this four-star hotel provides every creature comfort – large soundproofed bedrooms, luxurious rose-marble bathrooms, spacious public rooms, a sumptuous buffet breakfast served in the conservatory – but our inspectors found it lacking in individuality. Decoration adheres to an Art Deco theme. A predominantly business clientele is to be found seated at the smart black and pale wood bar.

■ 143 ave de Malakoff, 75116 Paris **Tel** (1) 53 64 52 52 **Fax** (1) 45 00 60 61 **Meals** breakfast, room service **Prices** 1,580-2,600F; standard double 1,800F; breakfast 110F **Rooms** 42; 39 double and twin, 3 suites, all with bath; all rooms have phone, TV, air conditioning, minibar, trouser press, hairdrier **Credit cards** AE, DC, MC, V **Closed** never

Seventeenth Arrondissement

North of Etoile

Hôtel Champerret Héliopolis

A surprising little hotel, decorated in beige and blue, sporting rust-coloured leather sofas, gold cushions and a line of multi-coloured cacti, with a refreshingly eclectic style. Though not large, the inviting reception acts as a sitting area and bar as well; guests eat breakfast perched on blue bar stools at the attractive pale wood bar, or sunk into one of the comfy sofas. Arranged around a tiny but pretty fern-filled courtyard, the bedrooms, in contrast to the ground floor, are disappointingly ordinary and spartan (all identically decorated in the same colour as the ground floor), but worth enduring for the low prices.
Nearby Arc de Triomphe; Champs-Elysées; Palais des Congrès.

■ 13 rue d'Héliopolis, 75017 Paris **Tel** (1) 47 64 92 56 **Fax** (1) 47 64 50 44 **Location** between ave de Villiers and rue Guillaume Tell; **parking** in street or blvd Berthier; **metro** Porte de Champerret, Péreire; **RER** Péreire-Levallois **Meals** breakfast **Prices** rooms 385-640F; standard double 450-595F; breakfast 38F **Rooms** 22; 12 double and twin, 8 single, 2 triple, all with bath or shower; all rooms have phone, TV, hairdrier
Facilities bar/sitting/breakfast area, patio garden, lift **Credit cards** AE, DC, MC, V **Children** accepted **Disabled** no special facilities, but access possible in garden rooms **Pets** accepted **Closed** never **Proprietor** Catherine Rennie

North of Etoile

Hôtel Regent's Garden

It has an English name, but this is a typically French hotel in a handsome shuttered mansion built by Napoleon III for his doctor. It is set well back from the road and, as you might expect from a glance at the exterior, has a glorious, large garden at the back, where ivy scales the walls, trees and flowering shrubs flourish, and tables and chairs are set out in summer. The interior has been done out in an appropriately country-house style with faded chintzes in the comfortable, still elegant *salon.* No one bedroom is the same; all are refined, with chandeliers and Second Empire chairs, upholstered in velvet or satin; some are vast, with two double beds; some, a little down-at-heel; all have modern bathrooms. If you are arriving by car, try to get here before 7pm, when you should have no trouble parking in one of the eight spaces in the hotel's forecourt.

Since our last visit new owners have taken over and much renovation has taken place. Reports please.
Nearby Arc de Triomphe; Champs-Elysées; Palais des Congrès.

■ 6 rue Pierre Demours, 75017 Paris **Tel** (01) 45 74 07 30 **Fax** (01) 40 55 01 42 **Location** between place Tristan Bernard and rue Marcel Renault; **parking** private outside hotel or car park in street; **metro** Ternes; **RER** Neuilly Porte Maillot, Charles de Gaulle Etoile **Meals** breakfast **Prices** rooms 710-1,400F; standard double 780F; breakfast 50F **Rooms** 39 double and twin, all with bath; all rooms have air conditioning, phone, TV, minibar, hairdrier **Facilities** sitting-room, breakfast-room, garden, lift **Credit cards** AE, DC, MC, V **Children** accepted **Disabled** no special facilities **Pets** accepted **Closed** never **Proprietors** Condy family

Seventeenth Arrondissement

Champs-Elysées

Hôtel Etoile Park

The sort of hotel which is full of exhausted tourists who like the fact that it is no more than a stone's throw from the Arc de Triomphe. The decoration is 'modern functional', with an elegant sitting area, and fairly appealing breakfast room, but the bedrooms lack character. New carpets throughout.

■ 10 ave Mac-Mahon, 75017 Paris **Tel** (01) 42 67 69 63 **Fax** (01) 43 80 18 99 **Meals** breakfast **Prices** 490-710F; standard double 680F; breakfast 52-72F **Rooms** 21 double and twin, 17 with bath, 6 with shower; 5 single with shower; 2 family; all rooms have phone, TV, minibar, hairdrier, safe **Credit cards** AE, DC, MC, V **Closed** never

North of Etoile

Hôtel Etoile Péreire

Well placed for motorists and air travellers, this hotel has been smartly done out in restrained modern style, with some split-level rooms; welcoming owners but soulless atmosphere.

■ 146 blvd Péreire, 75017 Paris **Tel** (01) 42 67 60 00 **Fax** (01) 42 67 02 90 **Meals** breakfast; room service (outside caterers) **Prices** 590-1,090F; standard double 690-790F; breakfast 54F **Rooms** 26; 5 duplex with bath, 15 double and twin with bath; 3 single with bath; 3 single with shower; all rooms have phone, TV, minibar, hairdrier **Credit cards** AE, DC, MC, V **Closed** never

North of Etoile

Hôtel Flaubert

A warm welcome from the hotel's owners and a luxuriant courtyard garden are the distinguishing features of this otherwise unexceptional hotel. Rooms one to ten have garden views; one to three have direct access.

■ 19 rue Rennequin, 75017 Paris **Tel** (01) 46 22 44 35 **Fax** (01) 43 80 32 34 **Meals** breakfast **Prices** 390-700F; standard double 550F; breakfast 40F **Rooms** 37, all with bath or shower; all rooms have phone, TV, minibar, hairdrier **Credit cards** AE, MC, V **Closed** never

Chaillot Quarter

Hôtel Régence Etoile

A 'listed' 1875 house, furnished in suitably traditional style. Improvements promised by the new management have begun, and half the generally spacious bedrooms have received a new colour scheme, mostly blue and yellow, and light, attractive bathrooms. There is more space for sitting than usual in Parisian bed and breakfasts.

■ 24 ave Carnot, 75017 Paris **Tel** (01) 43 80 75 60 **Fax** (01) 47 66 78 86 **Meals** breakfast **Prices** rooms 598-776F; standard double 776F; breakfast included **Rooms** 38 double and twin, all with bath or shower; all rooms have phone, TV, minibar, hairdrier, safe **Credit cards** AE, MC, V **Closed** never

Eighteenth Arrondissement

Montmartre

Style Hôtel

An 18thC building (opened as a hotel by the present owner's grandparents and little changed), not strictly speaking in Montmartre, but ten minute's walk away, full of character and with rock-bottom prices. All the bedrooms are spacious, and some are enormous, with huge windows, wooden floors, marble fireplaces and capacious old wardrobes. The simple bathrooms and shower rooms are modern and clean. The breakfast room has a provincial charm, with wooden tables, potted plants and fresh yellow walls. Though the ground floor lacks the style of the bedrooms, there is a pleasant courtyard and a fine staircase with wrought-iron balustrade. A great find for the low budget traveller.

Nearby Sacré-Coeur; place du Tertre; Moulin Rouge; place de Pigalle.

■ 8 rue Ganneron, 75018 Paris **Tel** (01) 45 22 37 59 **Fax** (01) 45 22 81 03 **Location** just off ave de Clichy; **parking** rue Caulaincourt; **metro** La Fourche, place Clichy **Meals** breakfast **Prices** 185-340F; standard double 285F; breakfast 22F **Rooms** 36, 2 with bath, 15 with shower, 19 with washbasin only (communal shower rooms/WCs in corridors); some rooms have phone **Facilities** breakfast room, courtyard **Credit cards** not accepted **Children** accepted **Disabled** access difficult **Pets** accepted **Closed** never **Proprietor** Geneviève Lescure

Ile-de-France

Barbizon

Hôtellerie du Bas-Bréau

Half of Europe's political grandees have been guests at this handsome and luxurious (Relais et Châteaux) inn. Seen from the road it looks small and chocolate box cute, but it extends back some 300 m, and includes two separate buildings. Of the rooms in the inn itself, one includes the Hirohito suite – sometime residence of the Japanese emperor. In the more modern building, which is set amid the beautifully tended flower gardens, rooms are decorated with restrained luxury in mind. Rich fabrics, discreet and subtle colours, capacious sofas, and up-to-date accoutrements, such as the Bang and Olufsen TVs. The dining-room has a reputation for excellent food, including delicious breakfasts, with plenty of choice.
Nearby Fontainebleu; Vaux-le-Vicomte.

■ 22 rue Grande, 77630 Barbizon **Tel** (01) 60 66 40 05 **Fax** (01) 60 69 22 89 **Location** in Barbizon, 60 km SE of Paris, 10 km NW of Fontainebleau, off N7; ample car parking, including private garage **Meals** breakfast, lunch, dinner, room service **Prices** rooms 950-2,800F; standard double 1,500-1,700F; breakfast 100F; menus from 400-800F **Rooms** 20 double and twin and suites, all with bath; all rooms have phone, TV, air conditioning, minibar, hairdrier, safe **Facilities** sitting-room, dining-room, bar, terrace, garden, swimming pool, tennis court **Credit cards** AE, DC, MC, V **Children** accepted **Disabled** no special facilities **Pets** accepted **Closed** never **Proprietor** M. and Mme Fava

Germigny L'Evêque

Hostellerie Le Gonfalon

The Hostellerie, which our inspector happened upon as he passed by one day, is set in a lovely wooded position on a bend of the River Marne, overlooked by a tree-shaded terrace, where a menu of mainly fish and seafood dishes is served in summer – or in the beamed dining room in cooler weather. Germigny-l'Evêque is aquiet residential village, but only 20 minutes from Euro-Disney, making it a perfect spot to escape to after a rigorous day in the land of make-believe.

Bedrooms on the first floor are large, each with the luxury of a private terrace, enclosed in winter, open in summer, and decorated in part with rather kitsch '70s style furnishings – you wonder where they managed to get them. Rooms above are more traditional. Madame Collubi, voluminous and in perennial bloom, has been in charge over the past 20 years.
Nearby Euro Disney; fMontceaux.

■ 2 rue de l'Eglise, 77910 Germigny-l'Evêque **Tel** (01) 64 33 16 05 **Fax** (01) 64 33 25 59 **Location** beside river Marne, in village, about 62 km NE of Paris, 9 km N of Meaux on D 97; car parking **Meals** breakfast, lunch, dinner **Prices** rooms 280-380F; standard double 320F; breakfast 50F; menus from 150F **Rooms** 8 double and twin, 4 with terrace, all with bath; all rooms have phone, TV, minibar **Facilities** sitting-room, dining-room, terrace **Credit cards** AE, DC, MC, V **Children** accepted **Disabled** no special facilities **Pets** accepted **Closed** Jan, Sun evening, Mon **Proprietor** Mme Collubi

Ile-de-France

Fontenay-Trésigny

Le Manoir

Our inspector found the exterior of this half-timbered, turn of the century mansion more 'Bavarian kitsch' than Norman English style, as it is meant to be. (It was originally built as a hunting lodge in the 19thC for a captain of industry and has been a hotel since 1950.) The interior is, however, distinctively French – rich and ornate in a 'glam-swag' way, and occasionally gloomy. Bedrooms differ widely in style: you could choose between, for example, a streamlined modern look, or a Japanese Samurai effect. Some rooms on the first floor have balconies overlooking the gloriously spacious grounds. Flying guests can land at the private aerodrome 30m from the front gate. Good classic cooking is served in the elegant dining room.
Nearby Vallée du Grand Morin; Vaux-le-Vicomte.

■ 77610 Fontenay-Trésigny **Tel** (01) 64 25 91 17 **Fax** (01) 64 25 95 49 **Location** in park between Fontenay-Trésigny and Coulommiers, off A4,52 km SE of Paris, 5 km N of Chaumes; ample car parking **Meals** breakfast, lunch, dinner, room service **Prices** rooms 900-1,300F; breakfast 70F; menus from 180-250F **Rooms** 20 double and twin, all with bath; all rooms have phone, TV, minibar, hairdrier **Facilities** sitting-room, 2 dining-rooms, bar, terrace, meeting rooms, garden, swimming-pool, tennis court, golf, fishing **Credit cards** AE, DC, MC, V **Children** accepted **Disabled** one room specially adapted **Pets** accepted **Closed** restaurant closed Tue **Manager** M. Sourisseau

Saint-Germain-en-Laye

La Forestière

The real charm of this sophisticated Relais et Château hotel is its romantic woodland setting. Arriving at the yellow painted house with brown shutters, trees and shrubs growing hard up against the front door and a riot of roses in the garden, it's hard to believe that you're still in a suburb of Paris. Bedrooms are as plush as you would expect though some of the decoration goes a tad over the top. The restaurant, 'Cazaudehore', has an excellent reputation and a fine cellar, and in summer tables are arranged along the garden paths, overlooking the immaculate flower-bordered lawns. In winter diners are warmed by an open fire. A peaceful walk along a series of bridle paths takes you from La Forestière to Château de Saint-Germain-en-Laye, the birthplace of Louis XIV, which now houses an archaeological museum.
Nearby Château de Saint-Germain-en-Laye; Château de Malmaison; Versailles.

■ 1 av. Kennedy, 78100 Saint-Germain-en-Layes **Tel** (01) 30 61 36 60 **Fax** (01) 39 73 73 88 **Location** in Saint-Germain-en-Layes off N184, 21 km NW of Paris; **parking** private car park **Meals** breakfast, lunch, dinner **Prices** 1,050-1,450F; standard double 1,050F; breakfast 75F; menus from 370F **Rooms** 25 double and twin, 5 suites, all with bath; all rooms have phone, TV, minibar, hairdrier, safe **Facilities** sitting room, restaurant, conference room, garden, lift **Credit cards** AE, MC, V **Children** accepted **Disabled** no special facilities **Pets** accepted **Closed** hotel never/restaurant Mon **Proprietor** Pierre Cazaudehore

Ile-de-France

Fontaine Chaalis

Auberge de Fontaine

A plain white building, formerly an *epicerie*, in a smart, isolated village in the middle of a forest, where the youthful owners have worked hard to create a simple, homely *auberge*. Rooms are beamed, comfortable and pleasantly higgledy-piggledy with good beds and terrific cast-iron baths. Very child-friendly.

■ 22 rue Grande, Fontaine Chaalis, 60300 Senlis **Tel** (03) 44 54 20 22 **Fax** (03) 44 60 25 38 **Meals** breakfast, lunch, dinner **Prices** rooms 265-545F; standard double 295-365F; breakfast 40F; menus from 135F **Rooms** 6 double and triple with bath or shower; 2 family with bath; all rooms have phone, TV **Credit cards** MC, V **Closed** Tues between Nov and Mar

Saint-Germain-en-Laye

Le Pavillon Henri 1V

Birthplace of Louis X1V, this is a building which has witnessed more romantic times than ours, and is now a small hotel, in the grand style, with sweeping views over Paris from the light and airy dining-room, the terrace and the front bedrooms.

■ 19-21 rue Thiers, 78100 Saint-Germain-en-Laye **Tel** (01) 39 10 15 15 **Fax** (01) 39 73 93 73 **Meals** breakfast, lunch, dinner, room service **Prices** rooms 450-1,280F; standard double 980F; breakfast 70F; dinner (à la carte) from 250F **Rooms** 42; 30 double, twin and suites, all with bath; 12 single, 3 with shower, 9 with bath; all rooms have phone, TV, minibar **Credit cards** AE, DC, MC, V **Closed** never

Senlis

Hostellerie de la Porte Bellon

A hostelry since the 16thC, found down a cobbled street in this lovely medieval town. Homely, very French interior with lots of heavy wooden furniture. Rooms in the old building have more character than the annexe, but lack en-suite bathrooms.

■ 51 rue Bellon, 60300 Senlis **Tel** (03) 44 53 03 05 **Fax** (3) 44 53 29 94 **Meals** breakfast, lunch, dinner **Prices** rooms 210-1,000F; standard double 400F; breakfast 35F; menus from 215F **Rooms** 19; 18 double and twin, 10 with bath, 4 with shower and WC, 4 with shower but no WC; one apartment; all rooms have phone, TV, minibar **Credit cards** MC, V **Closed** never

Confirming a booking

It is well worth booking a room in advance for the peak holiday seasons. Nowadays, many *chambres d'hôtes* have a fax which makes confirmation of a telephone reservation easier. The following is a simple letter that can be amended as needed:

Dear Sir, Madam,

I would like to book a room for two from ..... to ..... (dates) for ..... nights. Could you confirm the booking and the price of the room as soon as possible.

Yours faithfully,

....

(name)

Monsieur, Madame,

Je voudrais réserver une chambre pour deux personnes à partir du ..... au ..... pour ..... nuits. Veuillez confirmer la réservation et le prix de la chambre dès que possible.

Nous vous prions d'agréer l'expression de nos sentiments distingués,

....

(name)

Index of hotel names

In this index hotels are arranged in order of the most distinctive part of their name: very common prefixes such as 'Hôtel', 'Grand Hôtel', 'Hostellerie', 'Auberge', 'Relais', 'Le/La' and 'Au' are omitted, but more significant elements such as 'Villa' and 'Pavillon' are retained.

Index of hotel names

Index of hotel names

Index of hotel names

Menu decoder

A selection of the words and phrases that visitors find hardest to understand on Paris menus:

Abats	offal
Agneau	lamb
Aiglefin, aigrefin, eglefin	haddock
Aiguille	needlefish, garfish
Ail	garlic
Airelles	cranberries, whortleberries, bilberries
Allache	large sardine
Alsacienne, à la	with *choucroute*, ham and frankfurter sausages
Ananas	pineapple
Andouillettes	small chitterling sausages, usually served hot with mustard
Ange de mer, angelot	angel fish, resembling skate
Anguille	freshwater eel
Arachide	peanut
Araignée de mer	spider crab
Arapède	limpet
Ardennaise, à l'	usually with juniper berries
Arlésienne à l'	fish or meat with tomatoes, onions and olives
Armoricaine à l'	fish or lobster with brandy, white wine, herbs, tomatoes and onions
Baie de ronce	blackberry
Bar, badèche, cernier, bézuque, loup de mer	sea bass
Barbadine	passion fruit
Barbue	brill
Basquaise	with tomatoes, peppers and rice
Baudroie	monkfish
Bécasse, bécasseau	woodcock
Bécassine	snipe
Beignets	fritters
Belon	breton oyster
Bergère, à la	chicken or meat with ham, mushrooms, onions and potatoes
Betterave	beetroot
Bifteck	steak
Blanchaille	whitebait
Boeuf	beef
Bonite	bonito fish, resembling tuna
Bordelaise, à la	in red wine sauce with shallots, tarragon and bone marrow
Boudin noir	black pudding
Bouillabaisse	mediterranean fish stew
Boulangère, à la	oven baked, with potatoes
Boule de neige	sponge or ice-cream covered with whipped cream
Bourgeoise, à la	braised meat or chicken with bacon, carrots and onions
Bourride	white fish stew
Brandade de morue	dried salt cod mousse
Bretonne, à la	in onion sauce with haricot beans
Bretonneau	turbot

Menu decoder

Brochet	pike
Brochet de mer	barracuda
Broufado	beef stew with vinegar, capers and anchovies
Cabillaud	cod
Caille, cailleteau	quail
Camarguaise, à la	with tomatoes, garlic, herbs, orange peel olives and wine or brandy
Canard, caneton, canardeau	duck
Canneberge	cranberry
Cardeau, celan	sardine
Carrelet	plaice
Cassoulet	pork, mutton or lamb, cooked with haricot beans, bacon and sausage
Cèpe	wild mushroom
Cerise	cherry
Cervelas	smoked pork sausage with garlic
Cervelle	brain
Champignon	mushroom
Chasseur	with wine, mushrooms and shallots
Chèvre	goat
Chevreuil	venison
Chicon	chicory
Chou-fleur	cauliflower
Chou-navet	swede
Ciboule	spring onion
Citrouille	pumpkin
Civet	thick meat stew, thickened with blood
Clafoutis	baked cherry batter pudding
Colimaçon	snail
Colin	hake
Coquillages	shellfish
Coquille Saint-Jacques	scallops
Cornichon	gherkin
Cotriade	fish stew with onions, potatoes and cream
Couissinet	cranberry
Crécy, à la	soup with carrots
Crème Anglaise	egg custard
Crépinette	small flat sausage, encased in caul
Crevette	shrimp, prawn
Croque Monsieur	toasted ham and cheese sandwich
Crudités	raw vegetables
Cuisseau	leg of veal
Cuisses de grenouille	frogs' legs
Darne	thick fish steak
Daube	braised meat in red wine, herbs, carrots and onions
Daurade, dorade	sea bream
Dieppoise, à la	fish, often sole with shellfish, in white wine sauce
Dinde	turkey
Ecrevisse	crayfish
Encornet	squid
Epinard	spinach
Escargot	snail

Espadon	swordfish
Esprot	sprat
Esquinade	spider crab
Estouffade	pot-roasted met
Exocet (poisson volant	flying fish
Faisan, faisandeau	pheasant
Faséole	kidney beans
Faux-filet	sirloin steak
Fermiére, à la	meat or chicken braised with vegetables
Flétan	halibut
Fraise	strawberry
Framboise	raspberry
Galantine	loaf-shaped chopped meat, fish or vegetables set in natural jelly
Galette	breton buckwheat pancake
Garbure	soup with root vegetables and bacon
Gibier	game
Gigot	leg of lamb
Grecque, à la	mushrooms, aubergines and other vegetables poached in oil and herbs
Grenade	pomegranate
Groseille	redcurrant
Hareng	herring
Homard	lobster
Huître	oyster
Ile flottante	soft meringue on egg custard sauce
Italienne, à la	with pasta, tomato and mushrooms
Langue	tongue
Lapin	rabbit
Lièvre	hare
Lotte de mer, baudroie	monkfish
Lyonnaise, à la	with onions
Maquereau	mackerel
Marcassin	young wild boar
Merlan	whiting
Merluche	hake
Mirabelle	small yellow plum
Mode, à la	marinated meat braised in wine with bacon, calf's foot and vegetables
Mouclade	mussel stew
Moules	mussels
Mûre	mulberry
Myrtille	bilberry
Navarin	lamb stew with onions and potatoes
Navet	turnip
Niçoise, à la	with tomatoes, anchovies, olives and garlic
Normande, à la	with apples, cream, cider or calvados
Palombe	Woodpigeon
Palourde	clam or cockle
Pamplemousse	grapefruit
Panais	parsnip
Perdreau	partridge
Persil	parsley
Pintade	guinea fowl
Pipérade	scrambled egg with red peppers, onions and tomatoes

Plie	plaice
Pochade	freshwater fish stew with carrots and raising
Poireau	leek
Pomme	apple
Pomme de terre	potato
Pot-au-feu	boiled beef with turnips, leeks, carrots and
Potiron	pumpkin
Poulet	chicken
Poulpe	octopus
Poussin	baby chicken
Pouvron	sweet pepper
Praire	clam
Prune	plum
Pruneau	prune
Quenelle	poached, chopped fish or white meat, like dumplings
Raie	ray, skate
Ramereau, ramier	woodpigeon
Rave	turnip
Reine, à la	with chicken
Rillettes	shredded, potted meat
Ris	lamb or veal sweetbreads
Rognon	kidney
Rosbif	cold, rare beef
Rouget	red mullet
Salmis	game casserole
Sanglier	wild boar
Soupe au pistou	vegetable soup with basil paste
Tarte Tatin	upside down apple pie
Thon	tuna
Truffado	potatoes with garlic, bacon and chesse
Veau	veal
Vigneron, à la	in wine sauce,with grapes

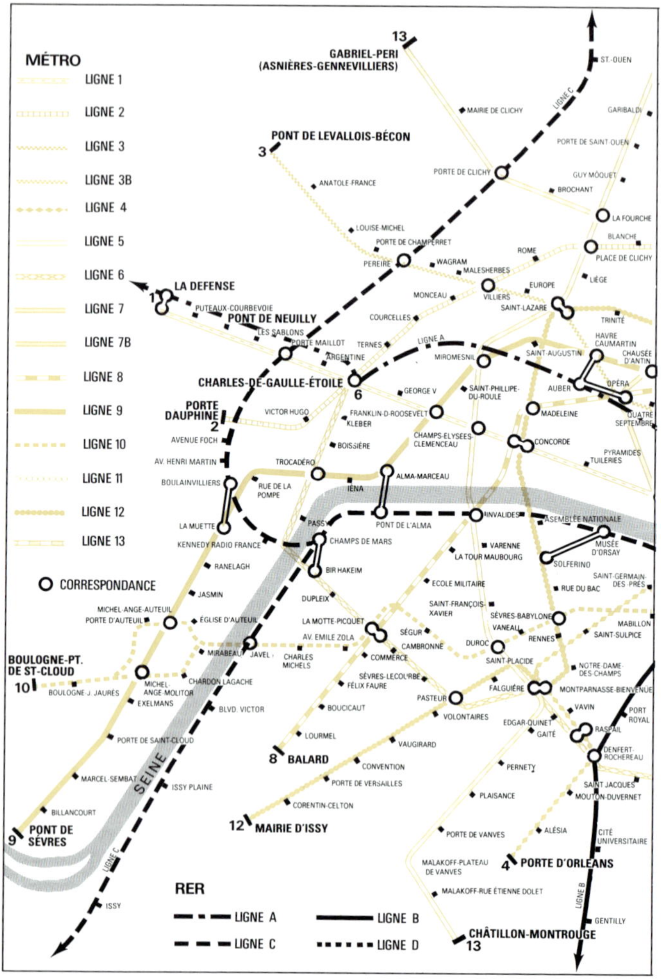
MÉTRO
LIGNE 1
LIGNE 2
LIGNE 3
LIGNE 3B
LIGNE 4
LIGNE 5
LIGNE 6
LIGNE 7
LIGNE 7B
LIGNE 8
LIGNE 9
LIGNE 10
LIGNE 11
LIGNE 12
LIGNE 13
CORRESPONDANCE
RER
LIGNE A
LIGNE B
LIGNE C
LIGNE D
GABRIEL-PERI (ASNIÈRES-GENNEVILLIERS)
PONT DE LEVALLOIS-BÉCON
LA DEFENSE
PONT DE NEUILLY
CHARLES-DE-GAULLE-ÉTOILE
PORTE DAUPHINE
BOULOGNE-PT. DE ST-CLOUD
PONT DE SÈVRES
BALARD
MAIRIE D'ISSY
PORTE D'ORLEANS
CHÂTILLON-MONTROUGE
SEINE
ST.-OUEN
MAIRIE DE CLICHY
GARIBALDI
PORTE DE SAINT-OUEN
PORTE DE CLICHY
GUY MÔQUET
BROCHANT
LA FOURCHE
ANATOLE-FRANCE
LOUISE-MICHEL
PORTE DE CHAMPERRET
PEREIRE
WAGRAM
MALESHERBES
ROME
BLANCHE
PLACE DE CLICHY
LIÈGE
MONCEAU
VILLIERS
EUROPE
SAINT-LAZARE
TRINITÉ
PUTEAUX-COURBEVOIE
LES SABLONS
PORTE MAILLOT
ARGENTINE
TERNES
COURCELLES
MIROMESNIL
SAINT-AUGUSTIN
HAVRE CAUMARTIN
CHAUSÉE D'ANTIN
AUBER
OPÉRA
QUATRE SEPTEMBRE
GEORGE V
SAINT-PHILLIPE-DU-ROULE
MADELEINE
VICTOR HUGO
FRANKLIN-D-ROOSEVELT
KLEBER
CHAMPS-ELYSEES-CLEMENCEAU
CONCORDE
PYRAMIDES
TUILERIES
AVENUE FOCH
BOISSIÈRE
AV. HENRI MARTIN
TROCADÉRO
ALMA-MARCEAU
BOULAINVILLIERS
RUE DE LA POMPE
IÉNA
PONT DE L'ALMA
INVALIDES
ASSEMBLÉE NATIONALE
MUSÉE D'ORSAY
LA MUETTE
PASSY
KENNEDY RADIO FRANCE
CHAMPS DE MARS
VARENNE
LA TOUR MAUBOURG
SOLFERINO
RANELAGH
BIR HAKEIM
ECOLE MILITAIRE
RUE DU BAC
SAINT-GERMAIN-DES-PRÉS
JASMIN
DUPLEIX
SAINT-FRANÇOIS-XAVIER
SÈVRES-BABYLONE
MICHEL-ANGE-AUTEUIL
PORTE D'AUTEUIL
ÉGLISE D'AUTEUIL
LA MOTTE-PICQUET
SÉGUR
VANEAU
MABILLON
SAINT-SULPICE
RENNES
AV. EMILE ZOLA
CAMBRONNE
DUROC
MIRABEAU
JAVEL
CHARLES MICHELS
COMMERCE
SAINT-PLACIDE
NOTRE-DAME-DES-CHAMPS
MICHEL-ANGE-MOLITOR
CHARDON LAGACHE
SÈVRES-LECOURBE
FÉLIX FAURE
FALGUIÈRE
MONTPARNASSE-BIENVENÜE
BOULOGNE-J. JAURÈS
EXELMANS
PASTEUR
VAVIN
BLVD. VICTOR
BOUCICAUT
VOLONTAIRES
EDGAR-QUINET
PORT ROYAL
RASPAIL
GAITÉ
PORTE DE SAINT-CLOUD
LOURMEL
VAUGIRARD
DENFERT-ROCHEREAU
CONVENTION
MARCEL-SEMBAT
PERNETY
PORTE DE VERSAILLES
SAINT JACQUES
ISSY PLAINE
MOUTON-DUVERNET
PLAISANCE
BILLANCOURT
CORENTIN-CELTON
PORTE DE VANVES
ALÉSIA
CITÉ UNIVERSITAIRE
MALAKOFF-PLATEAU DE VANVES
MALAKOFF-RUE ÉTIENNE DOLET
ISSY
GENTILLY

SAINT-DENIS BASILIQUE
(HÔTEL DE VILLE)
13
CARREFOUR PLEYEL
SAINT-DENIS
PORTE DE PARIS
LIGNE B.
LIGNE D
MAIRIE DE SAINT-OUEN
LA COURNEUVE-8 MAI 1945
7
FORT-D'AUBERVILLIERS
AUBERVILLIERS-PANTIN 4 CHEMINS
PORTE DE CLIGNANCOURT
4
PORT DE LA CHAPELLE
12
PORTE DE LA VILLETTE
SIMPLON
CORENTIN-CARIOU
BOBIGNY-
PABLO PICASSO
5
MARX-DORMOY
JULES JOFFRIN
MARCADET-POISSONNIERS
CRIMÉE
LAMARCK-
CAULAINCOURT
CHÂTEAU ROUGE
BOBIGNY-PANTIN
RAYMOND QUENEAU
RIQUET
ABBESSES
ANVERS
LA CHAPELLE
EGLISE DE PANTIN
STALINGRAD
HOCHE
PIGALLE
BARBÈS-
ROCHECHOUART
PORT DE PANTIN
OURCQ
LOUIS
BLANC
7B
SAINT-GEORGES
LAUMIÈRE
JAURÈS
GARE DU NORD
BOLIVAR
BUTTES-CHAUMONT
DANUBE
CHÂTEAU LANDON
BOTZARIS
PRÉ-ST-GERVAIS
7B
COLONEL FABIEN
NOTRE-DAME-
DE-LORETTE
GARE DE L'EST
MAIRIE
DES LILAS
11
POISSONNIÈRE
PLACE DES FETES
CADET
BELLEVILLE
LE PELETIER
PORTE
3B DES LILAS
RICHELIEU-DROUOT
CHÂTEAU D'EAU
PYRÉNÉES
JOURDAIN
TÉLÉGRAPHE
JACQUES BONSERGENT
COURONNES
SAINT-FARGEAU
BONNE NOUVELLE
STRASBOURG-SAINT-
DENIS
BOURSE
RUE
MONMATRE
GONCOURT
PELLEPORT
SENTIER
RÉPUBLIQUE
MÉNILMONTANT
PARMENTIER
PORTE DE BAGNOLET
RÉAUMUR-SÉBASTOPOL
TEMPLE
SAINT-MAUR
3B
GAMBETTA
3
GALLIENI
ETIENNE MARCEL
ARTS-ET-METIERS
FILLES DU
CALVAIRE
OBERKAMPF
PALAIS ROYAL
MUSÉE DU LOUVRE
CHÂTELET-LES-HALLES
PÈRE-LACHAISE
LOUVRE
RIVOLI
LES HALLES
SAINT-AMBROISE
PHILIPPE-AUGUSTE
RAMBUTEAU
SAINT-SEBASTIEN-
FROISSART
PONT NEUF
VOLTAIRE
ALEXANDRE DUMAS
CHÂTELET
11
HÔTEL DE VILLE
CHEMIN-
VERT
RICHARD-
LENOIR
CHARONNE
9
SAINT-PAUL
BRÉGUET-SABIN
BOULETS
MONTREUIL
AVRON
PONT MARIE
PORTE DE MONTREUIL
BASTILLE
2
MARAÎCHERS
CITÉ
LEDRU-ROLLIN
SULLY MORLAND
NATION
BUZENVAL
ST. MICHEL
FAIDHERBE-
CHALIGNY
PORTE DE VINCENNES
ODÉON
ST. MICHEL NOTRE DAME
SAINT-MANDÉ-TOURELLE
6
BERAULT
CLUNY
REUILLY-DIDEROT
PICPUS
LIGNE A
1
MAUBERT-MUTUALITÉ
GARE DE LYON
CHÂTEAU DE VINCENNES
LUXEMBOURG
CARDINAL LEMOINE
QUAI DE LA RAPÉE
MONTGALLET
BEL-AIR
JUSSIEU
DAUMESNIL
PLACE
MONGE
GARE D'AUSTERLITZ
10
MICHEL BIZOT
DUGOMMIER
CENSIER DAUBENTON
SAINT MARCEL
BERCY
LES GOBELINS
QUAI DE LA GARE
PORTE DORÉE
CAMPO FORMIO
5
CHEVALERET
GLACIÈRE
NATIONALE
PORTE DE CHARENTON
CORVISART
PLACE D'ITALIE
LIBERTÉ
CHARENTON-ECOLES
TOLBIAC
BOULEVARD MASSENA
LIGNE D
ECOLE VÉTÉRINAIRE DE MAISONS-ALFORT
SEINE
MAISON BLANCHE
PORTE D'IVRY
LIGNE C
MAISONS-ALFORT-STADE
MAISONS-ALFORT-LES JUILLIOTTES
PORTE DE CHOISY
MAISONS
ALFORTE
ALFORTEVILLE
KREMLIN-BICÊTRE
PORTE D'ITALIE
PIERRE-CURIE
CRETEIL-L'ECHAT
(HOP. HENRI MONDOR)
CRÉTEIL-UNIVERSITÉ
VILLEJUIF-LEO LAGRANGE
VILLEJUIF-PAUL VAILLANT COUTURIER
MAIRIE D'IVRY
7
VILLEJUIF LOUIS-ARAGON
7
CRÉTEIL-PRÉFECTURE
(HÔTEL-DE-VILLE)
8
©Oxford Cartographers

Reporting to the guide

Please write and tell us about your experiences of small hotels, guest-houses and inns, whether good or bad, whether listed in this edition or not. As well as hotels in Paris, we are interested in charming small hotels in: Britain, Ireland, Italy, France, Spain, Portugal, Germany, Switzerland and other European countries, as well as the east and west coasts of the United States.

The address to write to us is:

The Editors,
Charming Small Hotel Guides,
Duncan Petersen Publishing Ltd,
31 Ceylon Road,
London, W14 OPY
England.

Checklist

Please use a separate sheet of paper for each report; include your name, address and telephone number on each sheet.

Your reports are particularly welcome if they are typed and organized under the following headings:

Name of establishment
Town or village
Full address and post code
Telephone number
Time and duration of visit
The building and setting
Public rooms
Bedrooms and bathrooms
Standards of maintenance, housekeeping
Standards of comfort and decoration
Atmosphere, welcome and service
Food
Value for money

We assume that in writing you have no objection to your views being published unpaid, either verbatim or in an edited version. Names of major outside contributors are acknowledged in the guide, at the editor's discretion.

Special Offer

Buy your ***Charming Small Hotel Guide*** by post directly from the publisher and you'll get a worthwhile discount. *

Titles available:	*Retail price*	*Discount price*
Austria	£9.99	**£8.50**
Britain & Ireland	£9.99	**£8.50**
Britain's Most Distinctive B&Bs	£9.99	**£8.50**
Florida	£9.99	**£8.50**
France	£9.99	**£8.50**
France: *Bed & Breakfast*	£8.99	**£7.50**
Germany	£8.99	**£7.50**
Italy	£9.99	**£8.50**
New England	£8.99	**£7.50**
Southern France	£9.99	**£8.50**
Spain	£8.99	**£7.50**
Switzerland	£7.99	**£6.50**
Tuscany & Umbria	£9.99	**£8.50**
Venice & North-East Italy	£9.99	**£8.50**

Please send your order to:

Book Sales,

Duncan Petersen Publishing Ltd,

31 Ceylon Road, London W14 OPY

enclosing: 1) the title you require and number of copies

2) your name and address

3) your cheque made out to:

Duncan Petersen Publishing Ltd

**Offer applies to this edition and to UK only.*

Special Offer

If you like *Charming Small Hotel Guides* you'll also enjoy Duncan Petersen's ***Versatile Guides/Travel Planner & Guides:*** outstanding all-purpose travel guides written by authors, not by committee.

Titles available:	*Retail price*	*Discount price*
Australia	£12.99	**£10.50**
California	£12.99	**£10.50**
Central Italy	£12.99	**£10.50**
Florida	£12.99	**£10.50**
France	£12.99	**£10.50**
Greece	£12.99	**£10.50**
Italy	£12.99	**£10.50**
Spain	£12.99	**£10.50**
Thailand	£12.99	**£10.50**
Turkey	£12.99	**£10.50**

Please send your order to:

Book Sales,

Duncan Petersen Publishing Ltd,

31 Ceylon Road, London W14 OPY

enclosing: *1) the title you require and number of copies*

2) your name and address

3) your cheque made out to:

Duncan Petersen Publishing Ltd

*Offer applies applies to this edition and to UK only.